STANDING
ON THE WORD

Christian Educators in Public Schools

BOOKS

www.advbookstore.com

FINN LAURSEN

with commentaries by Dawn Marie Molnar

Standing on the Word by Finn Laursen
Copyright © 2015 by Finn Laursen
All Rights Reserved.
ISBN: 978-1-59755-319-3

Published by: ADVANTAGE BOOKS™
                 Longwood, Florida, USA
                 www.advbookstore.com

Library of Congress Catalog Number: 2015942743

First Printing: August 2015
15 16 17 18 19 20 21   10 9 8 7 6 5 4 3 2 1
Printed in the United States of America

Endorsements

In his many years as a Christian teacher, counselor, principal, and superintendent in the public school sector, Finn Laursen has encountered just about every issue and challenge one could imagine. In *Standing on the Word* he has selected a dozen issues that Christian educators are undoubtedly facing in schools right now, given a story of his personal experience with that issue, and then identified biblical principles and practices that will serve as an invitation to let God walk through those challenges with you. This is a book that will take you back to the basics of what you believe and encourage you to put those beliefs to work in overcoming people and circumstances that want to hold you back, discourage you, and keep you from living faithfully to your calling as a Christian educator who in many ways has been forced to live in exile.

Donovan L. Graham--BA, MA, Ed.D.*: Public secondary school teacher and counselor; Christian college professor, dean, and chaplain; director of the Center for Teacher Renewal; author of Teaching Redemptively: Bringing Grace and Truth Into Your Classroom, and Making a Difference: Christian Educators in Public Schools*

Finn Laursen writes a book for present, past, and future educators. Mr. Laursen speaks with wisdom and knowledge regarding experiences within the school place. He writes with honesty and candor about the environment, the situations, the people, and occurrences within the school setting. He captures the reality of the schoolhouse not found in textbooks. Mr. Laursen takes the reader on his personal journey including the mountain top experiences as well as the deep valleys (known to school teachers as the trenches). All of these experiences are first person and rooted in the Word and through the lens of a Biblical Worldview. Mr. Laursen's experiences will provide future educators with the reality of the school place and of the students and situations that could be encountered as well as how to handle these situations based on God's Word. The Parent's Commentary provides a parental perspective of the schools and how prayer and communication can provide both parent and teacher to more effectively meet the needs of the children/students under their care.

Yvonne D. Trotter, Ph.D., Associate Professor of Education, Geneva College, Beaver Falls, PA; CEAI Ohio State Director

---

Standing on the Word: Christian Educators in Public Schools takes an honest, yet uplifting look at what it's like to be Christian in a non-Christian environment. Finn shares his life stories that will resonate with any Christian educator who reads it, and all should.

Dr. Timothy Parson: *Principal of a public middle school, ordained elder and pastor in the Church of the Nazarene, adjunct professor at University of the Cumberlands.*

Finn's book challenges public school educators to not leave their faith at the schoolhouse door. This book equips Christian educators with the tools on how to legally live out their faith on a public school campus.

Dr. Bill Ziegler: *high school principal, Media Director for CEAI hosting the nationally syndicated radio program, TIPPS (Teaching In Public/Private Schools), served as the President of*

the Pennsylvania Association Elementary & Secondary Principals, on adjunct faculty at Temple University.

Do you have the facts? As a long time secondary school math teacher, I endeavor to teach the facts. If you want the facts about One: religious freedom in schools, Two: how to speak up for your faith, and Three: how to deal with contemporary issues in America's schools, then you must read ***Standing on the Word: Christian Educators in Public Schools*** by Finn Laursen.

Dr. Dean Finley: *high school math teacher, adjunct professor, and CEAI board member. He is a native to Springfield, MO. and currently resides there with his wife Helen; Graduate of Missouri State University and Southern Seminary; He has taught middle and high school, college, graduate schools, and seminary in five different states. He has visited more than 25 countries. He currently serves on the board of CEAI.*

It is my pleasure to recommend Finn's new book to you. As his older brother I want to affirm his credibility as a believer who lives out what he professes. Reading through this book, I was edified by the early stories of his life that have helped to shape who he is in Jesus. This brief writing is a summary of the core teachings that Finn has been sharing with Christian teachers since the 1980's when he established Master's Teachers Rallies based in northeast Ohio.

You have in your hands a book that has within it the DNA that can transform local schools and thereby powerfully shape thousands of students who will learn how to think rather than being programmed by what to think. This is an excellent tool for teachers, parents and board members who want to positively impact their local schools.

Paul N Laursen BA, MDiv, PhD: *Currently with AIMS, Colorado Springs; Pastoral Ministry since 1972 serving in Ohio and New York*

Finn Laursen is uniquely qualified to write this book: a compilation of subjects every teacher has had to or will face because he has lived each one himself. He does not shrink from lightening rod subjects, and does not hold back on how his Christian faith impacts every area of the school day. It will be a reference many teachers will turn to and study.

Bob Erdmann, *CEAI Board Chair, B.S. Mechanical Engineering from University of Missouri, Founder of Trinity Equipment, and author of The Call to Work and speaker on the marketplace and the theology of work.*

Finn Laursen is an example of an educational leader that exemplifies integrity. His wisdom and down-to-earth approach to educational concerns is practical, while still inspiring and motivating. I am honored to recommend this great resource as an effective additional tool for any educator.

LaRae Munk, *Director of Legal Services, CEAI. LaRae is a licensed attorney in Michigan. For the past 15 years she has developed an expertise in education law that has brought her national recognition. In addition, LaRae serves as school board attorney for more than 20 of Michigan's public school academies (charter schools). However, she believes her greatest achievement is her family—her daughter and grandchildren.*

Table of Contents

Finn Laursen

About the Author

The sun was rising over the horizon in the New York harbor as our massive passenger ship sailed past the Statue of Liberty welcoming our family of four to the United States of America. The Laursen family, consisting of my parents, older brother, and myself, was experiencing what most just read about in history books. In the early 1950's our immigrant family came to the shores of what my parents believed to be the *Land of Opportunity.*

My parents longed for the freedoms and opportunities they had read about in letters from family members already living in the U.S. They had personally experienced the oppression of the Nazi military that had overrun the Danish borders from Germany. The resistance lasted only hours. The citizens of Denmark resented the Germans and secretly resisted in many ways. My parents had joined that resistance as they worked with the underground passageway transporting Jews from Germany through Denmark to Sweden. As part of the resistance and at great risk to themselves, they had built a hidden room in their home to hide Jews.

Denmark was experiencing an economic depression in the wake of World War II. My father, a skilled bricklayer/stone mason, had been an independent homebuilder in Denmark. Having a challenging time supporting his family, my father took the advice of family members already in America. He packed up all he owned in two suitcases and a wicker trunk, and prepared his family for the long trip. My uncle, who was a successful farmer in Ohio, made all the arrangements state-side to allow us entry into the U.S. as well as provided temporary housing and support. This major change in the lives of the Laursen family was decided only after many hours in prayer seeking the Wisdom of the Lord. Once my father was confident he had a green light from the Lord and the support of his wife, he held a family meeting and plans were set in motion.

My pre-schooler mind was looking forward to going into America, believing it to be a single location or building. I kept bugging my parents to find out when we would get there, even as we walked down the streets of New York City. But my parents saw the United States as a place where they could share in a prosperity they had only read about: a country where hard work could lead to any level of success desired; a country where education was open to all; and a country that welcomed all who came to be part of this *great melting pot.* They expected to work hard, knowing their sacrifice would provide more opportunities for their two boys than they themselves had in Denmark.

Our entry into the States was less than a storybook delight! My brother Paul had not joined us on deck to take in the sights of this new land because he was recovering from emergency hernia surgery in the ship's hospital ward. Once we arrived in America, we spent our first days in a local hospital where my brother received post-op care. My parents seemed tense, but not panicked even though they knew no English and were in a foreign culture. When my brother was finally released from the hospital, family members arrived to take us to our new home in Ohio. Reality did not immediately live up to the dream of my parents. As a preschooler, I did not fully grasp the courage my parents had modeled for us. As I look back on this less than ideal entry into this country, I now realize the risk my parents took to uproot the family, leave home and extended family, and take on the unknown.

Once we were settled in Ohio, my father's priority was to find a job. He clearly had the strong European work ethic that drove him to be willing to do any kind of work. He applied for several types of work from farm labor to salt mining under Lake Erie. He was offered a job in the salt mines, which he reluctantly took so that he could support his family. However, two days before he was to head underground, God provided his dream job as a bricklayer (working above ground). He could not speak the English language, but he understood hard work, so he fit in well.

In Denmark, my dad's only mode of transportation was a bicycle, so he was used to riding a bike towing a tool trailer to his worksite; however, this was not doable in his new environment. With his first paycheck he bought a used car to use for work. The world of automobiles was new to him, but he learned quickly by driving on the dirt paths of the farm. He ran off the road a few times while learning to maneuver this huge vehicle, but his only victims were a few corn stalks. My dad was mechanically inclined, so he quickly learned how to care for and make minor repairs on his *junker*. However, no one ever clearly explained the importance of putting oil in the engine, an aspect of car care he discovered after the engine seized up. This was a great learning experience, and as a result this error was never repeated!

My parents worked diligently. My dad laid bricks for forty to fifty hours per week and then in the evening and weekends he took on the challenge of building homes for my uncle who owned farmland he wanted to develop. Over the next couple of years my father built two homes and used the extra income earned to purchase one of those homes for our family. My mother worked hard as well. She helped to harvest the crops in the fields of my uncle's farm in the summers and in the greenhouses in the winters. Despite her industrious work on the farm, my mother's first priority was being a wife and mother.

School opened a new world to my brother and me. We quickly learned a little English as we played with area children; however, these skills were refined as we entered the public school. This schooling opportunity was a part of my parents' American dream for my brother and me because the American public schools provided further education than would have been offered to us in Denmark. My parents only had the equivalent of a seventh grade education since the poor in Denmark were only provided a limited education. After his schooling, my father went on to become an apprentice bricklayer. My mother did what most in her social circle did - she went to live with a wealthy family to do housework and work in the fields, earning room and board along with a small stipend.

While we did all we could as a family to blend into the American culture, we maintained our Danish culture as well. We socialized with a circle of Danish families and acquaintances, keeping the language and culture alive for our family. We spoke Danish only at home or among other Danes and always switched to English when in public or when non-Danes were around. As soon as possible we became US citizens; until then we annually went to the post office to renew our green cards. Not all of our immigrant relatives jumped with both feet into the great melting pot. Some stayed off to the side without engaging in their new environment and, as a result, missed great opportunities.

My parents were clearly followers of Jesus. Although they were not outspoken about their relationship with God, my brother and I knew where they stood on issues of faith. Since they had been raised in the Lutheran Church, the National Church of Denmark, we naturally ended up in a Lutheran church in America. Much of our life was invested in the church and church activities. In fact, my brother, much to the delight of my parents, became a Lutheran pastor and earned a PhD. I too felt an attraction from the Lord and went off to college planning to follow in my brother's footsteps and become a Lutheran pastor. This fulfilled my parents' hopes and dreams of an expanded education for their sons – an education that they themselves did not have access to when they were growing up.

It was the late 60's and the Vietnam War was in full swing. I was so confident I wanted to go into the ministry that I pre-enrolled in the seminary and got my divinity student draft deferment. There was a move in the 60's in many of the denominations to *de-mythologize* the Bible, and the Lutheran college where I attended went full bore in that direction. After two years of religion classes designed to help me dig through the myths of the Bible to find some nuggets of truth, I realized that I had been taught out of whatever faith I had. I understand now that I only had *head knowledge* about the Lord that could be un-taught and not *heart knowledge…a personal relationship* with the Lord not dependant on understanding and proof, but based on faith. I knew I could not go any further in my quest to become a pastor just to promote a book of myths. My life had to mean more than that.

As I pondered my major change from pre-theology, I realized I wanted to help others. I often found myself being sought out for counsel by family and friends, which naturally led to becoming a school counselor. I have an internal drive to succeed, so I was successful in my schooling efforts in spite of the fact that I didn't enjoy it. I saw college as something I had to do. So I made the decision to switch my major to Education and focus on teaching the subject I disliked the least: English. At that time Ohio required three years of teaching before one could become a school counselor. I felt more compassion for older children so I became a secondary English major to fulfill the three-year teaching requirement to become a school counselor. I earned my Masters in Counselor Education during my first three years of teaching and in my fourth year became a high school counselor.

In year nine of my education career I had a *water-shed experience*. My wife Linda and I with our little daughter Dawn moved back to where we had grown up. We began to attend the same church I had attended as a child. I quickly realized something had changed in our church. I learned that our pastor had attended a Billy Graham Crusade, and he had been *born again*. The pastor spoke of being filled with the Holy Spirit. A new Gospel was being preached - one that I had not heard before. My brother, now in his fourth year as a pastor, told me he had a similar *born again* experience while watching a Billy Graham Crusade on television. At the time, I blew off his experience, considering him to be the weak family link needing such a crutch. Plus, I figured it was probably a good story for a pastor to tell. But something amazing happened - no something divine. What had seemed like foolishness to me began to make sense. Both my wife and I entered into a <u>personal relationship with our Lord and Savior Jesus Christ.</u> We experienced His Power, the Bible came alive to us, and our lives were literally transformed.

Shortly after coming to faith, our second child Michael was born. Even though my wife Linda had suffered with rheumatoid arthritis for many years and was heavily medicated, we thought the pregnancy had gone well. After my son was born, I noticed the nurses kept measuring the chest and the skull. I was devastated when the pediatrician told me Michael had liquid around his brain causing swelling of the head: a birth defect that can be caused by Linda's medication. While my son was still in the hospital, my brother was a guest preacher at my church. In the middle of his sermon, he stopped and announced that the Lord had just revealed to him that my son was healed. I was so fresh and naïve in the faith, I just accepted this with child-like faith. However, as I traveled to the hospital on Monday to discuss the treatment for the birth defect, I started having some doubts. Those doubts evaporated when the doctors stated that for some unknown reason the swelling in the skull had diminished, and they no longer saw a reason to move forward with any treatment. What a great introduction to the Power of our Lord!

At this time I was a middle school counselor in the public schools and felt it was time to make a career change. I felt so overwhelmed with the Truth that I could not go on as I had. It seemed logical to me that I should become a counselor at a Christian school so I could leave the heathens in public schools and be joined with the redeemed. I applied to every Christian school I could find, but I could not get a job counseling in one.

Being a true follower of Jesus was new to me, so it never occurred to me to pray about His direction for my new life. When I finally did consult Him through prayer, it all became clear to me. I had been called to full-time ministry like I had believed years ago. However, my parish wasn't a church. It was the public schools. Even though I did not initially realize it, God had already placed me in an environment to serve as a missionary. My career, my ministry, was about to radically change.

NOTE: Dawn Molnar has written a commentary at the end of each chapter in this book reflecting a parent's perspective on each topic.

About the Commentator
Dawn Molnar

I grew up in a very loving family. Early on, my parents and grandparents taught me the meaning of loving the Lord and having a relationship with Him. Not only did they tell me about the gift of salvation, but they also showed me what a life following Jesus looked like by the way they lived.

I attended a small Christian school kindergarten through twelfth grade. I was involved in sports, music programs, drama club, and various church programs. Even with all of that activity, I graduated valedictorian. You could say I was an overachiever.

I went to Grove City College, another small Christian school, where I studied English Secondary Education. I believe God has gifted me with a talent for teaching. I have a passion for it, actually. However, one of the reasons I was initially drawn to the teaching profession was because it was an ideal career for a parent – summers off, early hours, not many late nights working away from home... I had always wanted to be a mother, so my dream was to teach a few years and then start a family, focusing all of my attention on my children.

I married my college sweetheart a few months after college graduation. I was offered a teaching job near my hometown, and my husband was also able to obtain a teaching job in the same area. I felt totally blessed.

After five years of teaching in the public schools, my first child was born. My husband obtained a new job as a principal, allowing me to resign my teaching position and fulfill my dream of being a stay-at-home mom.

During my time off from teaching, I became a leader for my church's *MOPS* (Mother's of Preschoolers) group as well as collaborated to create and lead a *Teen MOPS* group, ministering to young moms. I also joined a *Mom's In Prayer* group, which meets once a week to pray for our local schools and our children. In the midst of this ministry to my family and community, I went back to school to earn my master's degree and license as a school counselor.

As I write this, I have three children: an eleven-year-old son, a nine-year-old daughter, and a six-year-old daughter. Now that all three of my kids are in public school, I have started to visit the classroom again through volunteering at my children's schools as well as subbing part-time. I also have begun teaching in several local *MOPS* groups, including my *Teen MOPS* group.

Even though I love subbing and my ministry, I still see my primary job is being a mother. My experience as a parent with children in public schools includes procuring a 504 plan, advocating for a gifted child not being challenged, and working with a child on focus and organization. Witnessing my husband's experiences as an administrator in several public school systems has given me a different perspective of education as well. Through my experiences, I feel I have gained great insight into the educational process. I hope that you are able to truly see what I have been privileged to observe in my role as a mom, and that God opens your eyes to a new perspective as you read my brief commentaries on the author's messages.

God bless you!

Preface

I shared my background with the reader in the preceding *About the Author* as I am confident that it has had great impact on me as an educator. However, the most prevailing impact on my role as an educator has to be coming into a personal relationship with Jesus. Once I realized that I could be in relationship with the living God, it changed everything. It truly transformed my life. What had once seemed like foolishness, suddenly made sense. I realized that God loves me and has a plan for my life even though I am sinful and had been separated from Him. Part of that plan is that Jesus died for me and thus bridged that gap for me. I reached out to the Lord with this child-like understanding and asked Him to be my Lord and Savior. I asked Him to guide my life and lead me into His will for my life. Once I asked Him to fill me with His Holy Spirit, the Biblical Principles outlined in this book came alive to me and made sense.

If you have not entered into a personal relationship with the Lord Jesus Christ, I'd encourage you to do so today. Your background, education, membership in a church, and your quest to understand life will be of no benefit without that personal relationship. If this makes no sense to you now, simply ask Him into your heart and be ready to experience the same transformation I did.

After understanding my call, my career exploded…in a good way. During my thirty-two year career in public schools I had the opportunity to serve as classroom teacher, a middle and high school counselor, an assistant principal at the middle school and high school levels, a high school principal, and a superintendent of schools. Those years ministering in the public school arena served as a training field for my position as Executive Director for *Christian Educators Association International*, a professional association focused on encouraging, equipping, and empowering Christian educators according to Biblical Principles.

This book will point to some of the powerful Biblical Principles I experienced during my sixty plus years within the public schooling culture as a student, teacher, administrator and executive director. Even though the focus of this book is on the public school, the same principles are valid in the private and Christian school cultures as well.

Throughout this book I share stories of my experiences, but at no time is it my intent to show any individual referred to in a negative light. To defer such focus I have changed the names of those alluded to and want to clarify that the stories are being shared to demonstrate a concept in the same fashion that fictional stories and parables do…the individuals involved are not the focus, but the truths demonstrated are.

Each chapter clearly reflects my perspective: that of an educator who is a follower of Jesus. I have invited a mother whom I highly regard as a dedicated parent, who is also a follower of Jesus, to write a commentary at the end of each chapter reflecting a parent's perspective. I know you will appreciate Dawn Molnar's insights since every child we serve has a parent we indirectly serve.

Since the purpose of this book is not that of scholarly research, I have not included footnotes, but include within the body of the writing written credit for data when important and unless marked differently have used the New American Standard version of the Bible for quotes.

This book can be used as a topical resource or read cover to cover. Questions are included at the end of each chapter and thus can be used for individual study and reflection or used in a group setting format.

I pray that you be blessed and encouraged as you read, ponder, and pray.

CHAPTER 1

Religious Freedom
&
Its Boundaries in Public Schools

[1] Let everyone be subject to the governing authorities, for there is no authority except that which God has established. The authorities that exist have been established by God. [2] Consequently, whoever rebels against the authority is rebelling against what God has instituted, and those who do so will bring judgment on themselves. Romans 13:1-2

It was early in the school year in my first year as high school principal. I was still quite a rookie and did not yet have a full grasp of what my new role would be. Our Art teacher Jon came rushing down the hallway after school clearly upset and anxious to get me out of the hallway so we could talk in private. My first thought was to ask him to wait until all the students had exited the building, boarded the buses, and were on their way home. However, the panic on Jon's face changed my mind. I walked him down to my office, shut the door, and gave him my full attention.

Jon nervously told his story, "Billy stayed after class this afternoon and asked if we could talk and I naturally said yes." He went on to explain that the student proceeded to close the door and then approached him behind his desk. Jon confessed that he had used poor judgment and clearly crossed the line. As I looked into Jon's watery eyes and saw his pale complexion I started thinking the worst.

I had been doing some counseling on the side for Children's Services at the time where I had been assigned to run groups for sexual offenders of children. As his story started coming together, it started sounding much like the stories these fathers, step-fathers, grandfathers, and uncles had been sharing in group. I started to feel panic setting in as I was thinking I had my first sexual abuse case as a principal. I had hoped for a positive start of the year, but it appeared that this was going to be a less than positive year.

Fortunately, my worst fears were unsubstantiated as Jon finished his story. When alone, the student simply asked if Jon believed there is a god. Jon said, "I did not stop and analyze, but simply answered yes...I now realize I violated separation of church and state and could lose my job."

I was able to explain to Jon that he broke no law because no law requires him to lie about or deny his faith. The courts have been quite clear that teachers do not lose their freedom of speech when they become teachers. Certainly they cannot use their positions to force their faith on their students, but teachers can answer questions if asked.

Jon was quite relieved...as was I.

I have found a growing belief among many educators that public schools must be religious free zones. Some have even gone out of their way to sanitize our public schools of anything that even hints of religion or faith.

It was not always so. Our forefathers birthed a nation based on Biblical principles and did the same when they formed public education. In 1789 the first Federal Education Law post-Constitution was passed. Our forefathers made it clear that public education in this new nation must be made up of three components: <u>Religion</u>, <u>Morality</u>, and <u>Knowledge</u>. They believed that religion was the basis for morality and if religion were removed, morality would soon collapse. They clarified that knowledge was important, but without religion and morality, knowledge could actually be dangerous.

These opinions were not just held by a few, but were generally accepted. Noah Webster, known as the *Schoolmaster to America* said, "Any system of education...which limits instruction to the arts and sciences and rejects the aids of religion in forming the characters of citizens, is essentially defective." Our first president George Washington said, "Reason and experience both forbid us to expect that our national morality can prevail in exclusion of religious principle."

Basically, they saw public education as a three legged stool balanced on <u>Religion</u>, <u>Morality</u> and <u>Knowledge</u>. As long as all three legs remained strong, public education in America would also remain strong.

High expectations were held for all students, and achievement soared. It was not unusual for students to move on to Ivy League Colleges in their early teens and even graduate from college still in their teens, ready to enter the workplace or serve in political office. Under this format, our education system became the envy of the world. We ranked first in Math, Science, and Literacy globally.

Then something happened in the early 60's. The US Supreme Court ruled that public schools were to be secular. They knocked one leg off the three legged stool of public education, leaving it balancing on only two legs: <u>Morality</u> and <u>Knowledge</u>. Over the next five decades our forefathers' prediction seemed to be prophetic. They had claimed that morality was built on the foundation of religion, and if religion was to be removed, morality would crumble...and crumble it did. The next generation of citizens held to no absolute truths, and morality as previously known was gone. Now the stool had only the leg of <u>Knowledge</u> left, rendering our educational system unstable and virtually ineffective.

Now the United States has dropped from first in Math, Science, and Literacy, and has continued to plummet downward along with the expectations of students. ACT and SAT scores have been re-normed twice because scores have continued to plummet.

The concept of denying the Christian roots of this nation is a new phenomenon. One I believe that has led many to deny their own faith and actually buy the lie that our public schools must be "God-free zones."

This belief actually contradicts the First Amendment of the Constitution. Our forefathers had great foresight when they penned the Constitution. They realized that building a strong nation could not happen without the help of the Lord. In the First Amendment they made sure that the government would not establish a religion nor prohibit the expression of religion.

At the Constitutional Convention Benjamin Franklin, perhaps one of our most liberal forefathers, set the tone for the writing. He realized that they had been meeting to draft a guiding document for a new nation and had neglected seeking the Creator. After the following speech overflowing with Biblical allusions, all future sessions were commenced with prayer.

On June 28th, 1787 Benjamin Franklin boldly said, "...I have lived, Sir, a long time, and the longer I live, the more convincing proofs I see of this truth- that God governs in the affairs of men. And if a sparrow cannot fall to the ground without his notice, is it probable that an empire can rise without his aid? We have been assured, Sir, in the Sacred Writings, that 'except the Lord build the House, they labor in vain that build it.' I firmly believe this, and I also believe that without His concurring aid we shall succeed in this political building no better than the builders of Babel."

As they penned the Constitution they assured that future government agencies, like schools, would not control religion or silence the convictions of a religious people. The First Amendment of the United States Constitution states, "Congress shall make no law respecting an establishment of religion or prohibiting the free exercise thereof...."

This Establishment Clause declares that no government agency can act in any way to establish a religion or do anything to stop the expression of religion. Thus the government cannot force religious beliefs on others, and cannot roadblock religious activity.

The Free Exercise Clause in the Constitution clarifies that the government cannot roadblock the freedom of speech given to those living in this great nation when it says, "....abridging the freedom of speech, or the right of the people peaceably to assemble, and to petition the Government for a redress of grievances."

With the First Amendment of the Constitution still in place, educators clearly do have some religious freedoms.

How would the First Amendment impact a public school teacher?

Public School Educators CAN:

- **Engage in personal prayer and Bible reading**
- **Attend student activities including prayer, Bible study, and worship**
- **Lead after school religious activities for students such as GOOD NEWS CLUBS**
- **Share personal religious beliefs when asked or when appropriate within curriculum**

- **Teach about religion or the Bible in curriculum**
- **Openly live according to their Biblically based convictions**
- **Share faith issues with staff**

Public School Educators CANNOT:

- **Use their position to promote their religious convictions**
- **Inhibit student religious expression**
- **Teach the Bible to students devotionally during the school day**
- **Lead students in prayer in their role as educators**
- **Treat religious expression differently than non-religious expression**

The courts have equated teachers as arms of the government since they are supported by public dollars. Thus a public school teacher cannot establish his or her religion in that classroom. In other words, the Christian educator cannot use their public position to force their beliefs on students. Conversely, the school staff cannot use its power to ban the free exercise of religion in the school.

For students in the public schools the First Amendment powerfully protects their freedom of religion. The school...or perhaps more clearly put...the public school employees can do nothing to abridge their rights. The school cannot inhibit the expression of religion. If students believe they are to share their faith with others, public school employees must step back and allow it as long as the students are not disruptive. If students believe they are to commune with the Living God via prayer…public school employees need to allow it. Bottom-line, if public school employees squelch the faith of students, they may well face the wrath of God as well as the courts. Such behavior by agents of the state (public school employees) would, in fact, fall into the category of religious harassment or discrimination. Public school employees should be hands off!

I would even suggest that perhaps they should just move out of the way when students boldly share their faith with other students in schools.

I'm reminded of the story shared by a mom of a public school student. This Christian first grade teacher made the most of a "teachable moment." One student unknowingly set the stage for another student to share the Gospel…all the teacher had to do was allow it.

This was the mom's story:

This Little Light

Story from a Christian mom

When my first born approached school age, my husband and I faced the ever-daunting decision: public or Christian school. We prayed and visited three schools, including our area public school. When after an extended period of time we didn't clearly hear a direction from God, we believed that God was leading our family to attend the public schools. Both my husband and I taught in the public school arena, and he is currently serving as a public school administrator, so we had some experience in that culture. Having been there, we were keenly aware that there would be amazing Christian teachers loving on our kids, but we were also aware that our children would face some real challenges that would test their faith. We also knew that our family could be an encouragement to their teachers and their classmates. Little did we expect that our little son's light would shine brightly so early on in his public school experience.

This year I had been really making an effort to encourage my son's first grade teacher. We were regularly emailing, and by October we were on a first name basis. She had made illusions to her faith to me, but I was not sure where she stood, so I didn't expect how God would use both her and my son to shine a light into the lives of his classmates.

I could hardly believe my eyes when I received this email from my son's teacher:

> *Hello again,*
>
> *We were watching a video about Christopher Columbus the other day, and it showed him praying to God for help when he was so discouraged and his crew was getting ready to mutiny. A little boy in the class said, "I wish he was still alive."*
>
> *I asked, "Who?"*
>
> *He said, "God."*
>
> *I said, "He is." I figured that I'd better shut up there and then.*
>
> *Your son took over. He agreed that He is alive, and explained that his son, Jesus had died, but he came back to life.*
>
> *What a touching moment.*

That is when the reality of where God had led us hit me – God had placed our entire family in the mission field, and my six-year-old son was witnessing with little to no effort. That mission field is our public schools. My son spoke up and shared about His Lord to a friend who didn't even know that God was alive. Then it also hit me that God had allowed my child to be in a classroom with a teacher who not only allowed him to express his freedom of religion in class, but who also shared our faith, and quietly cheered my son on without overstepping the boundaries placed on her as the teacher.

After experiencing this simple event, I believe that God has opened my eyes to the reality of our calling. He has called our family to be lights in the public schools. We are to be missionaries as parents when dealing with teachers, administrators, and staff. But it doesn't stop there. God has called my children to be lights to their classmates and teachers. In the same way, God has called you as teachers to shine by example and to open doors for the Christian kids in your classes to shine their lights as well. Once your students step out and begin to shine, be their cheerleaders, quietly praying for them and encouraging them behind the scenes. Imagine the glow all of our little lights shining together will create in our public schools!

We all get to play a role as missionaries in our public schools – parents, students, administrators, and teachers. I want to encourage us all to LET OUR LIGHTS SHINE BEFORE ALL, ESPECIALLY IN OUR PUBLIC SCHOOLS!

So there you have it. Teachers in public schools do have major religious freedoms while staying within the limits set up by the First Amendment. They certainly cannot create Christian classrooms...for that they would need to work in Christian schools; however, they can clearly impact the culture by openly living out their faith and encouraging other Christian educators, parents, and students.

Parental Commentary

As the mother who wrote "This Little Light," I can't emphasize enough the importance of Christian teachers knowing their First Amendment Rights as well as their students' rights. The teacher in my story handled this divine situation so well. She respected the boundaries set to protect the students from being indoctrinated by the government, while also respecting the freedom of her students to express their religious beliefs.

This situation could have gone a lot differently. When the child made the statement about God, the teacher could have panicked at the mere mention of God thus shaming the innocent student who asked that question. Or, the teacher could have interrupted my son and told him that he was not allowed to talk about God because of separation of church and state. My son would have felt that he had done something wrong, when, in fact, his religious rights would have been hindered.

But instead this teacher allowed my precious boy and his little friend to explore their beliefs together in a safe, non-threatening environment. No one was told they were wrong, and the truth of the Gospel was shared. Who knows what seeds were planted in the class?

I am so very grateful to that teacher who allowed my son to practice a major tenet of his faith: the great commission. Because he was not shamed and was allowed to help his friend, his faith grew.

Unfortunately, I haven't always had such positive experiences. When my daughter was in public preschool, each child in the class was to bring in something that started with the letter N. She insisted on bringing one of her favorite books – the children's

Bible that had a great account of the story of Noah. When she brought it in, I was nervous about how the teacher would handle it. She did allow my daughter to turn it in, but my daughter was told she wasn't allowed to read it to the other students because of separation of church and state. Unfortunately, this teacher was misinformed, and my daughter was basically told her N project wasn't as good as the others. I encourage you to not do this to your students.

I'm sure many of you will find yourselves in situations similar to the ones listed in my response and in this chapter. Be aware of the law and the rights of your students as well as your responsibility to protect them. Christian parents all over the country are entrusting you with their children, depending on you to not hinder or discourage their faith, especially as a Christian teacher. Maybe you have been called to let their light shine in the classroom along with yours.

WORKSHEETS

for personal reflection or group discussion:

What:

What principle(s) did I learn from the chapter?

So *What*:

How do these principles impact me?

Now *What*:

What action(s) will I take based on these principles?

What Happened:

What evidences do I or others see that these principles have impacted me?

Finn Laursen

CHAPTER 2

Submitting
to
Unreasonable Authority

[18] Servants, be submissive to your masters with all respect, not only to those who are good and gentle, but also to those who are unreasonable. [19] For this finds favor, if for the sake of conscience toward God a person bears up under sorrows when suffering unjustly. [20] For what credit is there if, when you sin and are harshly treated, you endure it with patience? But if when you do what is right and suffer for it you patiently endure it, this finds favor with God. 1 Peter 2:18-20

I was a new assistant principal at a middle school. This was my transitional year as I had invested the last eight years as a school counselor and this was my first attempt at being a building level administrator.

My role in this building was clear; I was in charge of all student discipline. My days were quite busy from before school to the end of the day... one student after another to deal with some type of challenge usually referred by a teacher...and they demanded some type of response.

One morning I found a note in my mailbox from Betty, a sixth grade teacher. The note said she was having a challenging week and asked if I'd pray with her over her lunch period.

I had been open about my faith so Betty knew where she could go for prayer, and I knew the legal limits of the law. I knew even assistant principals could take a lunch period even though I usually did not as my day was usually on overload with issues that could not wait. I knew that during my lunch period, my unassigned time, I could pray with a fellow staff member. I was not concerned that I might be breaking some law or ethical issue, but only wondered if I could be spared a crises from interrupting that half hour set aside for encouragement and prayer.

At 12:30 pm Betty showed up at my office, and I closed the door and met with her for a peaceful, uninterrupted thirty minutes. No one knocked at the door, and no one called on the phone during our time together…unheard of in my new role.

After our prayer time I went back to work as the hustle and bustle of the day came back to life. I did not get a chance to relax until the buses were pulling out of the lot at the end of the school day.

Then I got a call from the principal to come to his office. I felt like the little kid caught with his hand in the cookie jar and had no idea why I got the call.

When I knocked on his door, he asked me to come in and shut the door…I did not take that as a good sign.

The principal, Jeff, looked me in the eyes and asked, "Did you meet with Betty today during the school day and pray with her?" Unbeknownst to me, he had gone through my mailbox and read the note she had sent me. I explained to him that we had met during our lunch period and at her request we had prayed together. Although I had not planned to broadcast our prayer time, I knew I had not violated any First Amendment issue nor violated any state or local law or policy.

He pondered my response for a moment, pointed his authoritarian figure at me and yelled, "Don't you ever pray in that office with a staff member again!" The office grew silent, and I pondered my response. This was the second such command he had given me. Earlier that year, he called me at home after seeing a wall decoration that had a cross on it in my office. We had cinder block walls and the last assistant principal had left a nail in the wall that I used to hang a non-descript decoration that had a small cross engraved on it. Jeff had called me to explain that the cinder blocks were state property and therefore could not hold anything with a religious symbol. He demanded I remove it at once so that I not get sued. It was a silly issue that meant nothing to me so I explained at that time, that it was a simple decoration of little significance, but if it made him uncomfortable I would take it down. I explained that my life reflected that same cross, that I could not compromise, but the wall hanging was simply an attempt to cover an ugly nail.

But what was my response to be now? I knew he was wrong and could not forbid me to pray with a peer. As the Lord would have it, this weekend I was going to teach a lesson on submitting to authority at a youth retreat and the concept was clearly outlined in my mind. I was going to cast the vision for young people to submit to their parents even if they were unfair or unreasonable at times…as my boss was right now.

I held back the growing rage inside me, but instead calmly explained my understanding from a Biblical worldview of authority from the heavenly realms to church, family, government, and work. I went on to let him know I had not sought out the prayer time nor did I plan to do so in the future. However, this was clearly a God moment where we had a thirty minute uninterrupted time which just does not happen. If such a moment orchestrated by God happens again and I obey your order not to pray, would you then be accountable to God for my refusal to submit to His Directive to pray?

He was quiet for a moment as it seemed blood rushed out of his face. Then his finger of authority rose again as he said, "If you pray again, be sure to lock the door so people do not think we are running a cult here!" I promised to do so, realizing he had just given his blessing for me to pray in secret.

Six months later, Jeff stopped by my office without calling, knocked on the door, came in, and shut and locked my door. He tearfully requested, "The next time you...ya know...talk with God, please mention my wife. She was just diagnosed with breast cancer."

Had I demanded my rights six months ago, which had been an option, Jeff never would have brought me a prayer request.

Knowing our rights is a good thing. Being sensitive to the Holy Spirit on how to respond when our rights are violated is a priority.

For the next fifteen years or so, my right to be open about my faith within the public schools was not challenged. I was quite open about my faith as a high school principal and again as a superintendent of schools. My understanding of religious freedom in the public schools grew to the point that I regularly spoke at conferences around Ohio and beyond.

It seemed like I was being protected from any kind of attack on religious freedom issues. In fact, as superintendent of schools I did not work on Sundays so I let area pastors know that I could be available as a private citizen to cover their pulpits if they needed such. Within ten years I had preached in almost all the churches in my ninety-five square mile district...my faith was not in question.

I was what I and most others considered a successful superintendent....then one day a local wealthy businessman named Edgar got elected to my district's board of education. This man, unbeknownst to me, had declared that he was going to get rid of the Christian influence in the district starting with the superintendent…oh my!

He let me know in private that my career in the district was done, and he did all he could publically to demonstrate such. He challenged me at all board meetings and even regularly was published in area newspapers suggesting I was doing things inappropriately. Edgar demanded copies of my phone bills and copies of my emails, suggesting I was hiding something illegal. My office started getting a rash of demands for public documents, and at one board meeting our district's attorney of many years was dismissed without warning. Edgar informed me that all legal matters were now to go through a newly hired attorney who happened to be a friend of his. I was then asked to leave the meeting so the board could meet in executive session to discuss employees.

Out in the hall I could hear him yell to the attorney, "I do not care what his past evaluations say. I want that___ __ _ _____ out of here, and I want him out now!"

My life was no longer one of peace and success. Instead, it was stormy and tumultuous. I decided to start putting out resumes and interviewing for jobs elsewhere…that was when I realized the target on my back was bigger than I imagined. The day I met as a finalist for one of my potential jobs, my face was on the front page of the local paper with accusations of misuse of funds from Edgar…not true, but the district let me know that they did not want to get involved in this controversy and did not offer me the position.

Edgar was clearly setting me up at every turn, but I was convinced that I could not do battle with my boss, a board member, so I told him I would submit to his authority as long as he did not ask me to do anything illegal or immoral.

Even though my heart was not in it, I did not let the other board members know what was going on behind the scenes. Instead, I asked a group of men in my church to pray for my nemeses Edgar. It soon became obvious what was happening even though I did not expose it. At a public meeting two community members asked him if he was persecuting me due to my Christian faith, resulting in both community members being sued by Edgar. They endured two years of depositions.

In the meantime, area churches were incensed and started running candidates for the board. Before I knew it, I was offered a five-year extension on my contract, and my life changed once again.

Within six months, Edgar left the board and moved out of the system as the local papers started to uncover his many underhanded deeds. This included evicting a tenant in one of his rental homes who supported a school levy he wanted defeated in order to showcase me as a failure and poor leader of the district. We were back to having a positive school environment, and I had four years left on a contract that I was thrilled to fulfill in peace and harmony.

One day I got a call from an organization I had been volunteering with for many years…you guessed it…*Christian Educators Association International (CEAI)*. I had often wondered why I never landed any of the other jobs for which I had applied, and why I had to endure what I considered vicious attacks on my character and faith. I now realize being sheltered from overt attacks would not have provided the well-rounded experience needed for leading CEAI. Today when I meet with educators feeling persecuted and alone…I can relate, show empathy, and give first hand insight from a Biblical worldview.

The CEAI board asked if I would consider applying for Executive Director. It was a request I did not need to pray about as many years earlier I had already received the Call. Fifteen years prior I had started a ministry at my church to support Christian teachers in public schools. I developed and led many workshops and published a newsletter under the name *The Master's Teachers Rally*. One day while speaking at a teacher's conference, I shared the platform with Forrest Turpen, CEAI's Executive Director.

I said to Forrest, "I did not know there was a national association serving Christian educators since 1953."

Forrest Turpen, responded, "I did not know there was a superintendent in Ohio doing the same."

From that moment on, I served locally under the CEAI umbrella and continued to expand my legal expertise that has enabled me to testify as an expert witness in local, state, and federal courts.

I agreed to apply for the Executive Director position, which Forrest had filled for twenty years. I got the job, and as my first official act hired Forrest out of retirement to be part of our leadership team.

My experience in the trenches of public school education had its ups and downs as far as challenges go; however, one thing was clear. Submitting to authority was easy during the ups, but not the easy thing to do in the valleys. Regardless, Biblical principles are meant to be followed even when it does not feel good...and I found the Lord's blessings to follow every time...although that blessing was not always easy to recognize at the time.

Parental Commentary

Submitting to authority is a challenging attribute to master. My kids struggle with it every day. This concept resists comprehension to our selfish hearts. I still find myself struggling with the idea that I do not get to be in charge of everything.

However, as a parent, I expect my kids to submit to my authority. I use this example when they disagree with my directions or decisions. I remind them of when they were little and we would play in the front yard. We live on the main street of our neighborhood, so cars tend to go much faster than the allotted speed limit. This was rather dangerous for my toddlers who loved to chase balls into the street with reckless abandon. Before we would go out, I would review the guidelines of staying on the close side of the sidewalk. My kids would argue and I would remind them that I loved them and was making the rule to protect them, but they did not understand. Mostly they obeyed, but occasionally I would have to run out to the street to snatch them up, and we would have to finish our play inside. I remind them that they did not know why I made the "no play in the street" rule when they were little, but I knew something they did not. The rule was to protect them, not to harm them. Now that they are older they see why the rule was important. The same applies to the rules I make for them now. Just as they did not understand the "no play in the street" rule as a toddler, they may not understand the "no computer chat room" rule our family has now. I know something they do not. The rule is there to protect them, not to harm them.

As you work on submitting to your authority in the school setting, consider that your authority figure may know something you do not know. The decision or guideline you are struggling to accept may be there to protect you and not to harm you.

As a parent, I also struggle with my kids' anger regarding my decisions or rules. This can be extremely frustrating for me. One of the most grating sounds to me is whining. I cannot stand it! I actually find myself struggling with my own self-control when my three kids complain. When the bad attitudes become overwhelmingly evident, I usually start taking privileges away or become less apt to grant their next request.

As you work on submitting to your authority in the school setting, consider your attitude and the way your authority figure perceives your behavior. The way you approach the issue may have an impact on the respect you receive from your authority figure for quite some time. As a Christian, you may be the only vessel filled with the love of Jesus with which your authority figure comes into contact. We are called to be a city on a hill, salt, and light.

Believe it or not, I actually do make mistakes and sometimes my decisions are not the best for the family. Every rule I make is motivated by love, but occasionally my kids have valid arguments about why a decision should be tweaked a bit. If my kids approach me with respect and logically express their opinion rather than yelling, I am much more apt to hear the truth. I have had very productive, respectful discussions with my children, leading to a reversal of my previous rule or decision.

As you work on submitting to your authority in the school setting, consider the practical application of this principle in addition to the spiritual aspect of respecting authority discussed earlier. The reversal of bad decisions and policies is much more likely to happen if the idea of change is presented in a respectful, logical manner. There will be times when an authority figure makes a mistake, whether it be an administrator, school board, state policy, or national standard. The way in which you handle this mistake or bad policy will have great impact on how likely it will be corrected.

In conclusion, submitting to authority is a concept we Christians get to practice throughout our lives. We begin learning to submit to our parents when we are children, and we get to strengthen the skill throughout our adult lives with our bosses, law enforcement, and government. Our acknowledgement of the authorities' possible wisdom, our positive attitude, and the way in which we approach needed changes all showcase our mastery of this Biblical principle.

WORKSHEETS

for personal reflection or group discussion:

What:
What principle(s) did I learn from the chapter?

So *What*:
How do these principles impact me?

Now *What*:
What action(s) will I take based on these principles?

What Happened:
What evidences do I or others see that these principles have impacted me?

CHAPTER 3

God's Image

God created man in His own image, in the image of God He created him... Genesis 1:27

It was still early in my career when I accepted Jesus as my Lord and Savior and the Bible became alive to me. During this time it occurred to me that what I was doing as a counselor had no relationship to what Scriptures said. I started pondering whether I could counsel in a public school from a Biblical worldview.

For example, I wrestled with the concept that if we are all created in God's image, we are made with phenomenal creative potential that should be nurtured. Schools are often organized and managed with the sole purpose of controlling children, often squelching the natural creativity they have had since birth. As a middle school counselor, I often worked with students who were totally turned off to school. They had no interest in achieving and were convinced they were losers with no hope for the future. With no hope of success and no reason to comply with school restraints, they became the nightmares to the staff.

I had been trained in *Rogerian Counseling,* which stresses never directing the students counseled. If there are no absolute truths, non-directive counseling makes sense. Carl Rogers, the developer of non-directive counseling, believed that man was basically born good and if left to his own devices, good would come out. Along with many of his peers, he believed man could self-actualize and reach the full potential from within.

This contradicted what I was seeing in the Bible: that man had a sin nature and if left to his own devices, evil would come out. Man needed a Savior and could not do good on his own.

Once I made the commitment to be in relationship with the Lord and was filled with His Spirit, the Bible came alive to me, and I found absolute truths that could impact how I counseled students.

For instance, I was counseling a seventh grade boy, Billy. We all have known a Billy; he had no interest in school or achieving anything, so there were no incentives teachers could use to control his behavior or motivate him to learn. Billy was a continual disruption.

Billy had figured out the system. If you just refuse *to play school,* eventually you will be socially promoted to high school where you could hang out until old enough to quit school. With that goal in mind, grades meant nothing, and teacher approval was of no value. He soon understood that the most powerful punishment on hand was a suspension. He was regularly being sent to the office where the ultimate punishment, suspension, could be administered. In Billy's world, suspension was the desired outcome.

Eventually he spent more time in the guidance office than at the principal's office or in class. The principal had no more weapons in his tool box, and the teachers could not conduct orderly lessons with Billy in the room. He was hated by the teachers and not appreciated by the students who wanted to learn.

I decided I would try a different approach with Billy...a Biblical approach. I started treating Billy as if he was created in God's image and started seeing him through God's eyes: a young man full of potential. I not only treated him as such, I started verbalizing to him my high expectations for him. He was a clear leader and fearless in many ways. He was a gifted bully and a hero to many of the non-achievers who now had a role model to emulate. I was convinced that he clearly could be successful in any endeavor where he applied himself. I imagined him as a possible entrepreneur applying his gifts and talents to a successful venture.

On one of the rare days Billy was in class, I got a panicked call from the principal. He yelled, "Go to Billy's class…he is out of control…and run!" I'd never received a request quite like that so I ran.

What I found when I reached his class, still sends chills down my spine. The seventh grade class room was totally quiet…that alone was eerie. Over in the left hand corner of the room the teacher was pressed back in the corner with Billy approaching slowly holding a baseball bat over his head. The teacher was quite pale holding his hands out in front of himself in a defensive manner. Billy held the bat over his head saying, "I'm going to kill your _____ _____!" I had no doubt Billy was going to do damage. He had much pent up anger from negative interactions at school and an abusive alcoholic father at home. I later learned he was often smoking crack before school…not a breakfast of champions.

I walked up behind Billy trying to figure out what to do. I knew the non-directive counseling techniques I learned in college would not help. Engaging those would mean I should say, "Billy, how are you feeling …I see some aggressive tendencies are being exhibited today. What do you think might be the cause of those?" This would not save the day for the teacher or the students sitting in awe at their desks.

Knowing I had developed a relationship of respect with Billy and hoping this meant he would not hurt me, I yelled his name to get eye contact. I then approached, put him in a headlock and took him down. This spurred the teacher on to action to run up and take the bat away. Billy was a large, strong, young man who could have done damage to me, but refrained from doing so.

I got him down to the office where the process of expulsion was initiated. I did not need to lecture Billy, there were many who did that in the next few weeks, but I did respectfully walk him and his family through the process.

Years later as I was serving as a high school principal in another district; Billy showed up in my doorway...I recognized him immediately. In education thousands of students cross our path, but most we do not recognize years later. They seem to remember us, but it is often a challenge to hide the fact that we simply do not remember them. Often we remember the best and the worst, but even many of them fade after awhile.

Billy was not carrying a bat or weapon that I could see, so I invited him in. I was quite shocked to see him and wondered why he was here.

He told me his story of quitting high school and becoming a drug dealer, overdosing near death, and doing time in prison. He described himself as a successful dealer building a countywide network with a cadre of people working for him prior to his arrest. I found some consolation in knowing I had pegged him correctly as having entrepreneurial potential. He told of laying on his prison bunk one day and wanting to die when he started to remember some of the things I told him in middle school. That very day he invited Jesus into his life and transformation started.

While counseling Billy during middle school, I had not broken any law, but merely showed Billy the transformational love of God and answered any questions he asked about my faith. He always had a hard time understanding why I treated someone like him as if he mattered.

He said he had waited six months after his release from prison to look me up wanting to make sure his conversion *stuck* outside of prison. He wanted me to know that my efforts with him had not been in vain. Billy admitted that he often acted as if he was not listening, but he had heard everything I said and studied how I treated him and others.

I had been struggling in my role as a Christian educator working in the public schools. I often felt a lack of fruit from my efforts and I had started to wonder if my call was over. I then realized that those of us playing the role of missionaries in the public schools often plant seeds that may take years to bear fruit and be ripe for the harvest. Often, we would never witness the harvest from the seeds we were planting, but that planting was a requirement for the harvest by others to take place.

What Billy had not realized is that he had as much an influence on my life as I had on his.

Treating our students as if they are created in the image of God could revolutionize our teaching and other interactions with our students. Not only will our classrooms flow differently than if we are attempting to force control over our students, but we may be making an eternal impact on the lives of our students. If we polled our students, most likely many of them would report that they do not feel that the adults in their lives treat them with respect. What would happen if you respectfully treated your students as if they were created in the image of God?

When I implemented this Biblical worldview, my life was forever changed, and I know at least one of my students' lives was changed as well.

Parental Commentary

This was it - the first day of school for my first child. That morning, I could hardly believe my little one was going to spend his days with another woman teaching him, comforting him when he hurt himself, correcting his misbehavior, and, hopefully, championing his accomplishments. We took video and a dozen pictures at home, at the bus stop, and getting on the bus. I could hardly contain my tears as he waved from his bus window.

I joined a group of anxious moms as we jumped in our cars to try to beat the bus to the elementary school. I parked my car and sprinted to the doors of the school, clutching my camera. As the wind was blowing through my hair, images of my child as an infant and toddler flashed through my mind. It was difficult to accept that I was giving a major portion of influence over my child to another person – his teacher.

With a smile, I greeted him as he disembarked the bus. A few of his classmates were already crying, making it even more difficult to control my own emotions. We walked hand-in-hand down the hallway toward his new home away from home. I helped him find his nametag, unload his book bag, and take a seat. I got a big hug and smile from my little one, and I left him all too soon with a wave of my hand.

That was it. In a few minutes I had transitioned my little one into the hands of his teacher. He is one of my greatest treasures, and I was placing, and still do place a HUGE amount of trust in my son's teachers. Each day when he gets on that bus, I am sending him into another world where I can't look after or protect him. That job belongs to his teachers.

The crazy thing is that I had to go through the same thrilling yet painful day with each of my three children. And to this day I pray that their teachers see them as the amazing children they are. I guarantee most of your students' parents are also hoping that you treat their kids with respect, like the treasures filled with potential that they are.

Sadly, in my experience, not many teachers actually treat their kids as if they were created in the image of God. They have policies to follow, rules to enforce, and educational integrity to uphold. However, my children are not numbers in a mass of cattle. They are bright, fun, unique masterpieces molded by the same hands that created you. I desperately pray that their teachers treat them as such.

I guarantee there are many moms like me, who would ask the same from you if they knew they could trust you to accept this request without prejudice. How would your teaching style change if you saw each child as a creative being? How would your evaluations change? How would your classroom management change? How would you talk to your students even when you are having a bad day or they are super irritating?

Moms like me want to know and are counting on you...

WORKSHEETS

for personal reflection or group discussion:

<u>What:</u>
What principle(s) did I learn from the chapter?

<u>So *What*</u>:
How do these principles impact me?

Now *What*:

What action(s) will I take based on these principles?

What Happened:

What evidences do I or others see that these principles have impacted me?

Finn Laursen

CHAPTER 4

Missional Educators

But seek first His kingdom and His righteousness, and all these things will be added to you. Matthew 6:33

I was in my seventh year as an educator sitting in the teachers' lounge listening to my peers moaning about how many years they had left until they could be set free in retirement and start enjoying life. I even heard some Christian educators privately saying they longed for the day they could become involved in ministry to youth rather than be a teacher in a broken secular system: their perception of a Godly goal for retirement. They talked of all the challenges they faced daily, and I started feeling overwhelmed as well: being under staffed; over-worked; unappreciated; and overloaded with mandates from central office, the state department of education, and from DC. To make matters worse, the economy seemed to be in a downward spiral, student test scores were not improving, and we even seemed to be experiencing increasing health issues in our community.

Then it happened!

I entered into a personal relationship with the Lord, and my focus changed. I became a missional educator. I would like to say that I got off my knees and this change of *seeking His Kingdom* as priority one happened instantly, but it was a process of learning and growing as I decreased and He increased within me. The challenges themselves did not change, but I became *mission minded* and started focusing on others rather than myself. I still had challenging job responsibilities to perform, but my energy was focused on Kingdom issues: being the source for releasing God's Love and Truth in my schooling culture. It became about our Lord and those in my sphere of influence who needed to experience Him through me; therefore, I became a *missional educator*. I stopped focusing on getting out of my secular setting and focused on how the Lord would have me be His transformational agent within that setting. His Kingdom became more important than my comfort, and I found that my new focus changed lives and even brought victory to situations that on my own seemed overwhelming.

When I started to consider my schooling environment as my mission field, it did not look so overwhelming. I could stay in my own home, in my own country, speak my own language, and live in the affluent culture I have become accustomed to. I realized other missionaries were called to live lifestyles of unbelievable sacrifice making my mission field look pretty awesome. I always had the thought that someday the Lord might call me to risk my life on a foreign mission field, but even as of today, mine is the mission field of public school where my life is not at risk. The biggest risk might be going beyond my comfort zone…and possibly losing a job…not life or limb…in order to stand by my convictions.

As a nation we have a history to be proud of when it comes to public education. In the 19th century we could boast of having the first free public school system in the world. In the 20th century we made the biggest investment in higher education in history through the GI Bill, thus creating the most educated, knowledgeable citizenry the world had ever known.

Along with this educational "explosion" came economic growth that helped move us into the position of a world power. Our citizens experienced economic prosperity that became the envy of the world. Our educational system and affluence drew droves of immigrants from other nations wanting to partake of the American dream.

In fact, I was a child of one of those families and thus can speak from personal experience. In the 1950's my parents along with my older brother and I immigrated to the United States hoping to experience that affluence. My parents worked hard to build a future and saw their two sons flourish in the public school system with my brother becoming a pastor and me an educator.

Any level of change requires action of some kind. From a missional perspective, we can focus on our students with love and grace beyond our own capacity. We can help transform them by assisting them to become all the Lord created them to be. As we treat them as valuable creations of our Lord, we can foster levels of success they never could have imagined before.

The influence of missional educators certainly has spiritual implications as students see glimpses of Jesus through the educators' love and grace extended to them, but there are other measurable *earthly* impacts as well that go far beyond the contents of the curriculum they unfold for students. The success we can encourage students to experience in the schooling process can impact their future economic status and even health and longevity.

As educators we can facilitate positive change in the socioeconomic potential of our students. The level of education that a person completes is one of the main determiners of income. Many of our potential school dropouts could be coaxed toward success in school if they experience the kind of love and grace that can only come through a missional educator: one who refrains from treating them the way they deserve to be treated.

Education Determines Earnings

Median Earnings for Population Age 25-64 by Education Attainment, 2006

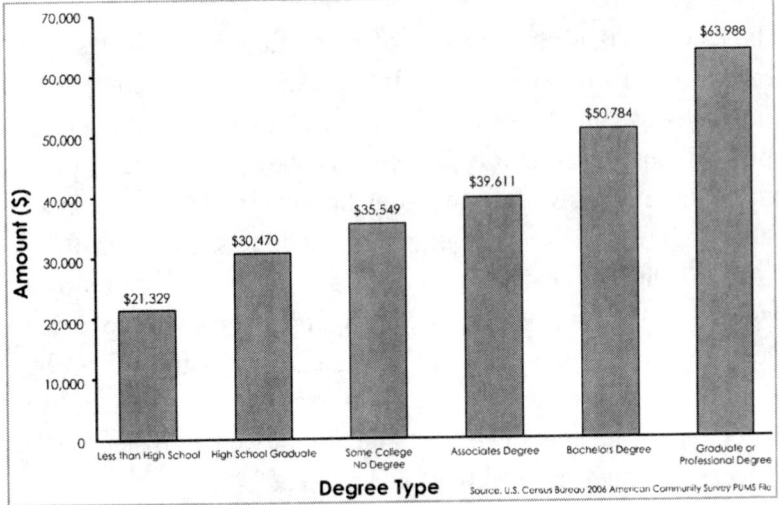

As educators we can impact the future physical health of our students as well. Health curriculum has for a long time focused on the importance of healthy lifestyles that lead to longevity - from the food we choose to eat or not eat to our recreational activities and even our sexual choices. Certainly what we teach and role model has impact, but statistics verify schooling success alone has impact as well. As we encourage our charges to succeed, health may follow.

Education continues to be one of the major forecasters of success in our nation and can even be linked to longevity. Studies reveal that level of education not only impacts the financial situation of an indivdual but also impacts health. It can be verified that the higher level of education a person has, the longer he or she may live; more education equals better health and thus longer life.

More Education, Longer Life

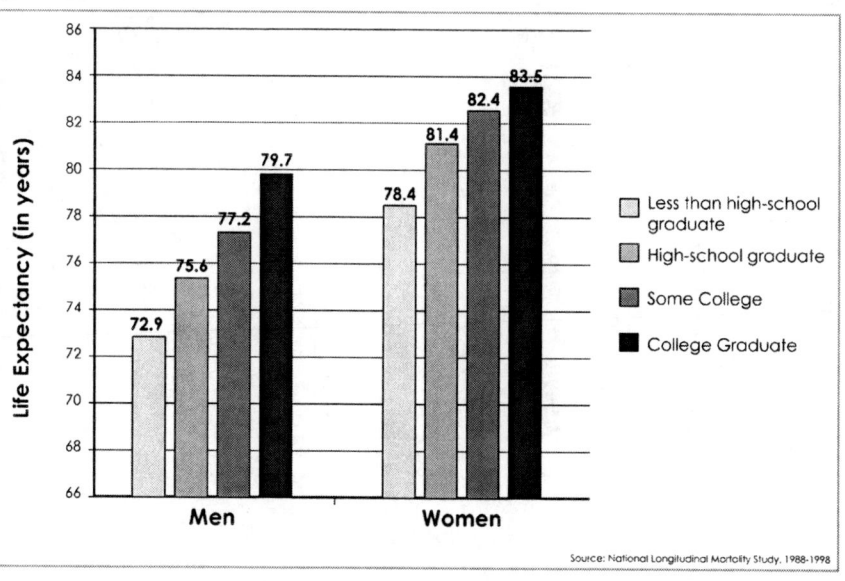

Source: National Longitudinal Mortality Study, 1988-1998

The impact we can have on our students reaches into future generations. Reviewing some statistics based on education level reflecting the reality of the parents whom we serve certainly can predict what we can expect from our students as they reach adulthood, and there is no reason to believe their reality will be different from their parents. Looking at the children of this same generation of adults can certainly also help us predict the impact of education on them and future generations of children.

The health of children also hinges on the education level of their parents. The more education parents have, the less illness is found among their children.

More Educated Parents, Less Illness among Children
Percentage of children, ages 17 and under, with poor/fair health

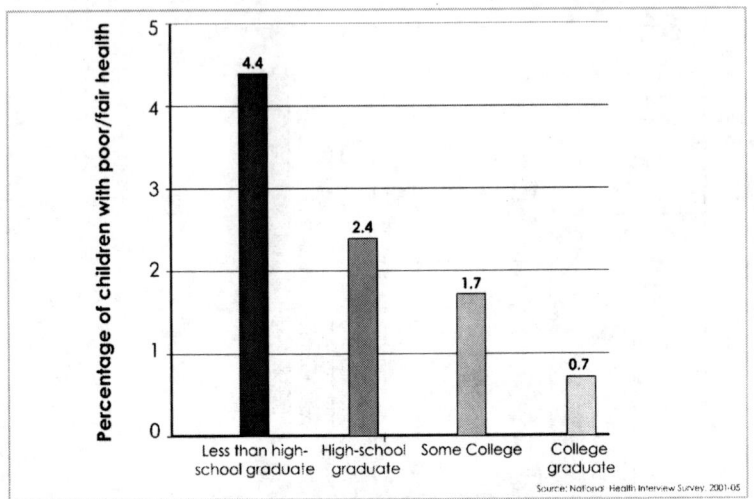

Source: National Health Interview Survey, 2001-05

   The potential impact of a missional educator is awe inspiring. Being the source for releasing God's Love and Truth in the schooling culture can bring transformation now and into the future. The transformation in the lives of our students we seek cannot be brought about through a financial bailout from Washington; many of our urban schools are drowning in cash flow and still continuing the downward spiral. It is not more school reform that continues the cycle of promoting the latest fad that those of us who have been around long enough have seen before under a different banner. It is not simply more accountability by increasing the already overload of testing for students and test results for teacher accountability.

   If it were that simple we would pump billions of more dollars into education, mandate the best practices that work and force more testing and accountability penalties.

I am convinced that our hope lies in the Lord through the hundreds of thousands of Christian educators investing their lives in our public schools.

We need TRANSFORMATION! Just as the Lord has transformed our lives, He can do the same as we bring the Holy Spirit with us to our schools.

Although the task of transforming our schools nationwide seems overwhelming, one person at a time, one day at time, can start the process.

Consider the changes that could take place if Biblical Truth ruled among our students: others being more important than ourselves, work being as "unto the Lord," forgiveness and compassion being the norm, the Power of the Holy Spirit being a daily observance, etc.

With all of our Lights turned on high, the Lord working through us can make TRANSFORMATION a reality one child at a time, one classroom at a time, one school at a time, one district at a time, one community at a time, one state at a time, and finally as a nation transformed from a self-centered humanist nation, we can become the shining light on a hill leading the world toward TRUTH AS GOD SEES IT.

Too ambitious? I think not. With God all things are possible.

Will you make a difference by being a *missional educator* with a focus on TRANSFORMATION?

Parental Commentary

The impact you as a teacher have on the future economic, physical, and psychological health of your students is pretty impressive. When the dividends of positive influence on future generations are added to the equation, the investment you make in your students seems like a very sound investment.

As a mom, I know what it feels like not to see the dividends of your investment initially. I can't tell you how many temper tantrums, loads of dirty laundry, and messy rooms I have experienced. Nights with little sleep nursing a newborn, days spent holding a sick child, and early mornings helping a middle school student prepare for a big day at school can seem draining with little to show for my investment of time. I labor all day, washing all the dishes and all of the laundry and by the evening of that very same day the sink is full of dirty dishes and the hampers are again overflowing. However, I know that I am investing in my children. This concept is what helps me not quit despite the feeling of futility I often experience. Each load of laundry shows how much my children are loved. Each night spent rubbing the back of a sick child is evidence of God's tenderness toward my child.

Don't get me wrong, my house isn't filled with rainbows and butterflies. My kids still make mistakes, and if I was honest with you, I would admit I actually hate doing the dishes. However, every once in awhile I see a glimpse of the return on my investment in my children – my son tells his friend about Jesus; my daughter stands up to a bully at school who is tormenting a classmate; my youngest daughter says she wants to be like Peter in the Bible and follow Jesus. I thrive on these little glimpses of the dividends I am investing every day into the lives of my children.

I understand that the classroom can also seem discouraging just like my dirty dishes and never-ending laundry hamper. Another call from an annoying parent; a student who calls you a name you have to look up on the internet; a student who never seems to come to school or finish an assignment can be so very discouraging. However, I challenge you to watch for glimpses of the dividends resulting from your investment in your students. The more encouragement and modeling of positive choices you shower on them, the greater the chance you will see glimpses of these qualities in your students. The more you invest into the lesson plans and pursue excellence in your academic and teaching practices, the greater the chance you will see glimpses of this type of effort from your students. I bet if you keep your eyes and ears open, you will see a glimpse of the dividends of your investment.

The impact my investment in my children will have on future generations in my family almost brings me to tears. I am leaving a legacy for my family whether I am conscious of it or not. My goal is to have my great grandchildren tell their grandchildren about how I lived a life for God. I want them to aspire to follow in my footsteps, following Jesus, totally in love with Him. I want them to invest in their children in the same way that I invest in mine.

The impact your investment in your students will have on future generations should have some type of effect on you as well. You are leaving a legacy for your students whether you are conscious of it or not. I challenge you to be conscious of your example of work ethic, academic excellence, virtues, showing God's love to others through service and words, etc. Don't you want your students to tell their kids about the teacher who encouraged them to make good choices, who told them they have potential to make the world a better place, who showed them the importance of academics and hard work, who demonstrated God's love to them? The author showed you statistics that prove you can reap dividends on your investment in the classroom long after you have left this earth.

This seems like a sound investment to me. I hope you invest with boldness and reckless abandon. Go all in for Jesus!

WORKSHEETS

for personal reflection or group discussion:

<u>What:</u>
What principle(s) did I learn from the chapter?

<u>So *What*:</u>
How do these principles impact me?

Now *What*:
What action(s) will I take based on these principles?

What Happened:
What evidences do I or others see that these principles have impacted me?

Finn Laursen

CHAPTER 5

Boldness, Courage and Daring

For I am not ashamed of the gospel, for it is the power of God for salvation to everyone who believes, to the Jew first and also to the Greek. Romans 1:16

I sat in the witness box in federal court in Florida wondering what I would be asked by the *American Civil Liberties Union* (ACLU) attorney who slowly approached me with a smirk on his face. His question, "Have you ever heard of the Great Commission?" My attorney had coached me to only answer what was asked with as few words as possible and not to go beyond the question.

"Yes," I responded.

"What does it mean?" he went on.

"It was Jesus' command to share the Gospel with others...to share the Good News."

The attorney moved closer as if coming in for the kill and asked, "Do you believe in the Great Commission?"

I gave my well trained answer, "Yes."

As he stepped closer, he asked, "Do you encourage the members of *Christian Educators Association International* (CEAI) to practice the Great Commission?" Now his plan was clear. He wanted to make me admit that we encourage them to proselytize as public educators thus violating the Establishment Cause.

I looked him in the eyes and responded, "We encourage them to openly, but legally, live out their faith, never crossing the line established by the First Amendment."

I felt that I had avoided his trap, but he continued to barrage me with accusatory rhetoric and one by one placed into evidence documents he had gleaned from the internet, quotes I had made in CEAI's *Teacher's of Vision* magazines and our e-newsletters. All dealt with not being ashamed of the Gospel and not going into a closet to hide our faith from others. My explanations continued to assert that living out our faith often did not even take words, but simply actions lining up with Biblical principles and sometimes simply refraining from certain behaviors such as gossip and slander against others...even those who might deserve negative reactions.

One might ask how I ever got in the position to be grilled by an ACLU attorney.

I almost hesitate to write about the situation out of fear this book would be classified as fiction and placed in the fiction section of libraries. The reality of what happened in the *Santa Rosa School District* in Florida seems too hard to believe...perhaps more of a reality in a third world nation or in a country where communism rules...but it happened right here in the land of the free.

The ACLU was on the lookout for school districts that pushed religious freedoms beyond what the Constitution allowed. Once they found violations, they would file a lawsuit against such districts. With mega dollars behind such efforts, districts cringed when such lawsuits were filed, as it often carried huge costs for districts. If districts were found guilty of such miscarriage, they not only could be hit with punitive damages and huge defense costs, but also would be charged back the attorney fees of the offended parties. In this case, the ACLU had up to four attorneys at their table and two rows of support staff in the gallery. I could almost hear the cash register totaling up huge sums as I sat at our table occupied my just one attorney and me. The ACLU now was offering to drop such suits if districts would agree to their terms in a settlement.

To try to keep such costs to a minimum, districts often signed off on what is called a *consent decree* where certain demands were agreed to. The school district in this case signed off on such as they had been guilty of violating the Establishment Clause. Overzealous Christian staff prayed openly with students and even had prayer broadcast over the PA system. The ACLU filed suit on behalf of two students who had been exposed to such violations, and the dollars started flowing. When the ACLU offered a way out of the court action that had been started in federal court, the district signed to stop the financial bleeding, which to this point was already in the multi-millions.

Many in the district did not realize the details within this document, but panic arose once the truth leaked out. For instance, employees were not allowed to pray while on school property whether on duty or not, whether during the school day or not. They were told, for example, that if they were at an athletic event, even as a community member or parent, they could not pray. The decree even went as far as demanding they stop others from praying as well, even if such a violator was a pastor. If this was not enough to shock a person of faith, the decree forbade staff from even giving the appearance of prayer by bowing of the head or folding of the hands. Staff was warned that if they violated any demands of the document, and I have but mentioned a few, they would face contempt of court charges and face possible time in jail.

Christian Educators Association International got involved when some of our members contacted us to ask for help from this oppressive court supported decree. We petitioned the federal court to enter this debate as we felt it violated the Constitutional rights of some of our members. That was how I ended up on the stand as did some of our members…just wanting for them the same rights teachers had in other districts. We felt the district did not have the right to sign away what the Constitution guarantees its citizens. I frankly thought the battle would be easy, but it was not to be so.

Days were spent in depositions that included many of our members who displayed the boldness, courage and daring to go public for their rights. Keep in mind that their superintendent had signed the agreement to make the ACLU go away, and now we were bringing them back into the court. This time it was the ACLU and the district against CEAI and some individual teachers that were not ashamed of the Gospel and willing to fight those opposed to the freedoms others enjoyed in public schools across the nation. I remember one of our members who cried on the stand as she told of being at a sporting event as a parent when her son was injured. She ran to comfort him realizing once she got there, the decree made it illegal to pray for her injured son.

Just in case some employees did not take the restrictions seriously, the ACLU charged one of our members with contempt. We had to defend her in federal court as she faced the potential of jail time for what the ACLU claimed were serious charges against her. She had been at an awards banquet off school grounds at an event not sponsored by the district, but included many school employees. When it came time to say grace, she was befuddled. Quite frankly, she had not been given enough clarity on her restrictions to be sure if she was allowed to pray, so she elbowed her husband and asked him to pray as he was not a school employee. That's right…that elbow and encouragement to pray got her in front to the judge and sent chills of fear down the spine of other believers not wanting to face the wrath of a federal judge for simply living as a believer in what they had until this time believed to be the land of the free.

This court action and others surrounding this case brought many to their knees in prayer, and every day as we walked into the courthouse, we saw fellow believers demonstrating across the street, praying, and singing songs of praise as we faced the challenges in the court room.

Although our battle did not end with the consent decree being totally thrown out, it was amended to return the First Amendment rights to the educators and support staff in the Santa Rosa District.

After I thought all was over, I took a deep breath and was thankful we had fought the battle for our members and that so many of them took the risk to defend religious freedom in their own back yard. However, it was far from over as CEAI was served with documents where the ACLU demanded we now pay their legal fees since we instigated our members to illegally live out their faith in the public school. We fought this latest attack as a non-profit, without the funds to pay off the ACLU beyond what the school district had already done. It was once again David fighting Goliath.

The good news…besides the Gospel…is that we prevailed and owed the ACLU nothing financially. However, I did owe them for some great insight gained through the process. I learned the importance of not giving into bullies, even if bigger and seemingly stronger…at least financially. I learned the importance of being willing to defend the religious rights of others. If we let their rights be taken away, ours are bound to be next.

I had never imagined myself in a court room facing a federal judge and the ire of an ACLU attorney. After all, I am merely an educator and a man of faith not wanting to cause anyone any harm. Yet taking on the boldness, courage, and daring that I believe was provided by the Holy Spirit, we helped set free the employees of a school system that tried to sign away the freedoms for which many have fought and even died.

I would encourage us all to be bold, courageous, and daring when it comes to our faith. I encourage us to stand up to those who may appear to be "bigger" than us who might attempt to take away our freedoms. I would encourage all…not to look for a fight…but not to be ashamed of the Gospel and to speak out and fight when necessary.

If we do not, who will?

Parental Commentary

I would love for my children to have a good role model. There are so few of them available for my kids. The few I gave my children the OK to watch on television, or buy their music, have for the most part publically gone off the path I hope my kids will follow as they mature into adulthood. Honestly, most parents would agree that having a role model reinforce the character traits being taught at home is a huge asset.

How cool would it be if my kids were in contact on a daily basis with a man or woman who had high moral standings and fought to hold true to them? Very Cool!

How excited would I be if a man or woman who influenced my kids advocated for them when the system they are forced to be a part of isn't working toward their best interest? Extremely Excited!

How inspired would my kids be if they witnessed a man or woman stand strong in a commitment or belief? Powerfully Inspired!

How amazing would it be if you were that person – their teacher? Truly Amazing!

What are you waiting for? Be bold, be courageous, and be daring for your Lord and your students. They are watching you!

WORKSHEETS

for personal reflection or group discussion:

<u>What:</u>

What principle(s) did I learn from the chapter?

<u>So *What*</u>:

How do these principles impact me?

<u>Now *What*</u>:
What action(s) will I take based on these principles?

<u>*What* Happened:</u>
What evidences do I or others see that these principles have impacted me?

CHAPTER 6

Words We Speak

Let no unwholesome word proceed from your mouth, but only such a word as is good for edification according to the need of the moment, so that it will give grace to those who hear. Ephesians 4:29

It was the start of another busy day in the life of a public school superintendent. I was reviewing my calendar of commitments for the day and surveying the huge stack of documents my administrative assistant so politely placed in front of me. Before I had an opportunity to entertain a feeling of being overwhelmed, I got a phone call from the teachers' union president.

She sounded agitated as she insisted I bring Mary (one of our middle school teachers) back to work. Mary was out on maternity leave...not my doing...and the union chief was demanding I bring her back to the middle school now!

I was a bit befuddled by the request, as maternity leave was an employee benefit and the union president was demanding me to rescind it, something I'm confident she knew I could not do. Plus, if I did, I'm sure a grievance would be filed for violating our negotiated agreement by the very same union president.

The union leader went on to explain why they needed Mary back at work. She said, "Mary is, you know, one of those Bible people." I acknowledged that I knew she was a Christian as she never kept her faith a secret. The union leader went on to explain that the staff loved her, and out of respect for her, they stopped using four letter words in the teachers' lounge.

A reality in the schooling culture is that the teachers' lounge is often a place where the staff comes to complain, vent frustrations, and whine. It is often a place where students are maligned, families dissected, administrators crucified, and where words of death overflow…words that wound, kill, and destroy. Over the years many teachers have told me that they avoid the lounge, as it drains them of energy and hope. Many leave there discouraged and depressed.

The union president explained that this was the state of their lounge until Mary arrived. The first to go was the foul language…not because Mary complained, but it was evident by her unwillingness to join such banter that she did not approve.

Next she stated that every time someone put down a student, family, or administrator, Mary brought some positive aspects into the dialogue. Eventually the negative talk stopped, knowing that she would just put a positive spin on the negative intent. Even though her positive spin on all things irritated a few, the cut-throat discussions ultimately ceased, and the middle school teachers' lounge transformed into a place to go in the middle of the day to be refreshed and renewed. A place of hopelessness became a place of hope by the words of just one teacher among many. Mary simply applied a Biblical principle and changed the culture of the teachers' lounge.

Finally, the union president said that without Mary the lounge had gone to <u>hell.</u> She quickly apologized for the use of the word, but I assured her I had heard the word before and understood her frustration. She explained that first the obscene words returned because no one was there to offend. Then the negative talk took over. She said that going to the *Mary-less* lounge was now a draining and debilitating experience. Rather than a time to refresh for the rest of the day, the lounge reinforced hopelessness, and some had again resorted to hiding out in their classroom to avoid the devastation.

Not wanting to pull Mary away from her new baby any earlier than necessary, I did not share the union president's concerns with her at that time. However, upon her return within her timetable, I did share with her the positive impact she had on the staff and encouraged her to keep making a difference.

It should not surprise us that what we say has an impact. After all, we are created in the image of God, and our God spoke the universe into existence. Life exists only because our Lord spoke it to be. What we say likewise can produce life or the opposite: death. What we say to our students can make all the difference in the world.

I remember very few of my elementary school experiences, but one incident is as clear as if it happened yesterday. Second grade posed quite a challenge for me, and I hated when the morning came and I had to go to school and be humiliated another day. In fact, I started getting nervous stomach aches after supper in the evening since I knew the next day was on the horizon. I did poorly in any class where reading and language were involved...which included most of them. On my report cards my teacher wrote, "Speaks foreign language at home."

Having been born in Denmark, we always spoke our native language of Danish at home. It being the original language of all in our family, it was just natural to speak it and express ourselves that way. Unlike languages you memorize and translate in your mind, Danish was the language in which I thought naturally...and even the language I dreamed and day-dreamed in.

I did not understand the significance of the language comment on my report card, but I did understand the significance of my low grades...I obviously must be stupid and of little value compared to my peers, many of whom blossomed at school and were appreciated by each other and, most importantly, by the teacher.

One day the unthinkable happened. Inside my report card carrying a D in English was a note from my teacher to my parents: "Please schedule a conference with me to discuss your son's progress in school."

I dreaded it when the day came for my parents to take me to school for this conference. The schooling culture and the language was still a bit foreign to my parents, so they invited my older brother Paul to come along…great, now he would know what a failure I was too. Paul was three years ahead of me in school and was excelling. My parents figured he could help translate or figure out what the school wanted them to do.

I still remember the shocking words of my teacher. She reassuringly said to my parents, "Finn is a good little boy, and I want you to know that he will do well in school. He has gotten some low scores on some tests as he is acclimating to the language; however, I have watched him work, and I can promise you that things will turn around for him. He will do well!"

As she went on to brag about my potential and explain to my parents not to be concerned about my grades, I kept wondering if she was talking about another little boy. I watched the sense of pride beaming from my parents' faces as my mom reached over and grabbed my hand. I walked out of that meeting floating on a cloud believing I truly might make it in this world. You see, that second grade teacher spoke words of hope and words of life into my being, and it has made a huge difference.

Interestingly enough, fifteen years later, I walked into a classroom as a teacher. Not just any type of teacher, but an English teacher. Along that successful route, my parents often reminded me of those prophetic words of my second grade teacher, "Things will turn around for him, and he will do well!"

Often the words we speak or how we communicate with our students are more important than the material we teach or the rules we attempt to enforce.

As a middle school counselor I remember one day sitting in the office of Frank our assistant principal just taking a few minutes to relax and share while getting away from our busy schedules. He and I were laughing and telling funny stories of our experiences thus far that school year. Our current status could best be described as two educators enjoying a few minutes of non-productive fellowship.

We were interrupted by a knock at the door. Frank went through a total physical metamorphosis to prepare for the student on the other side of the door. The man who had been relaxed in his chair, sat upright, changed the smile to a scowl, and adjusted his relaxed voice modulation to a grouchy tone before telling the student to come in. I watched as the negative exchange continued until the business of the meeting with the student was over. Once the student left and the door was shut, the nice guy returned on Frank's face and in his voice.

It was that day when I started wondering if one could be nice to students, show them respect, use encouraging language and still maintain the discipline teachers need to be successful. It was actually that observed behavior that led me to go back to school to get my administrative licensure, believing I could implement the principles of Ephesians 4:29…using words that edify and give grace …while not compromising on school discipline.

I actually ended up on the other side of the desk where Frank had been sitting and replaced him as assistant principal at the middle school. I got to test my theories of how best to use words when communicating with students…even those choosing to live out negative behavior. It should not be surprising that Biblical principles work…even in public schools. I served as the building disciplinarian both at the middle school and later the high school level and found that indeed one did not need to act in an adversarial role to maintain positive discipline. In fact, I found great success avoiding such roles. I'm not suggesting that students will at all times embrace discipline when handed down, but when wrapped in respect and positive words, it is like adding sugar to medicine...it goes down easier and the desired end result is often better.

This principle was even found to work in the process of teacher evaluations. Certainly there are times when negative comments are needed to help teachers improve, but they are easier to accept after pointing out some of the positive aspects a teacher exhibits. Principals are only as successful as their teachers are in the classroom so it just makes sense to applaud the things they do well so they can be encouraged and the achievements reinforced can continue. If the area needing improvement can be wrapped in some positive language, it is easier to accept.

I tried an unusual technique on the high school staff when reviewing daily lesson plans. When I saw something extra creative, I took a chance and used scratch and sniff stickers. I saw how much fun my children had with those at home and gave it a try...it was a great hit. In fact, teachers started keeping track of who got the most. Positive input with a twist of humor...like extra credit!

I also remember mentoring a principal who was frustrated that his staff always argued with him about his evaluations and continually filed rebuttals rather than focusing on improvement.

I reviewed his evaluations and found the majority of them to be negative and critical. When I reviewed one such evaluation with him, I asked him if he was planning to fire this teacher. He said, "No, she is one of my best and I want to help her refine her teaching to become even better. We can all improve...even our best!" I suggested he reevaluate her and put that in written form. Spend most of the document letting her know she is one of the best and why. Once you have edified her, built her up, she might be willing to look at the speck of an area to improve. Teachers are often underappreciated and evaluations, both formal and informal, are great opportunities to appreciate them.

In conclusion it is important to realize that what we say is often more important than what we think or do. Words are powerful motivators and words are powerful destroyers. Scripture likens the tongue to a rudder of a ship; it is small, but controls the direction of a large ship. In the same way we can set the course of all the lives in our sphere of influence merely by what we say to them or about them. The sphere might include, students, peers, authorities, and parents. The greatest litmus test before letting words roll off the tongue is to ask the question, "Will this be an encouragement and provide grace to the situation or individuals involved?" If the answer is yes...let the tongue roll on...if no, bite the tongue. We have filters that can screen our computers; we need to apply a filter to what we say as all our words have POWER...after all, we were created in His Image and His Words have Dynamite Power.

Parental Commentary

I have seen teachers' words wield power in the lives of my kids. The second and third grade years for my son showed evidence of how powerful the attitude and words of a teacher can be.

In second grade my son started bringing home bad grades on papers. You need to know the personality of my son to understand the magnitude of this issue. At age two he asked me to teach him to read. I rebuffed this only to have him beg on a regular basis. Finally, I agreed to help him learn his sight words. He was reading chapter books by kindergarten. As he grew, I had to force him to play and reward him for playing with time to read and study. He thrived by learning, and he loved to teach himself. By age five he had memorized the bones and sections of the brain. He could tell me all about whichever body system he decided to focus on and had researched himself. His desire to learn never stopped; just his interests would change. In short, my son loved learning and going to school.

When my son started second grade, he was a little sponge, excited to learn and never a behavior problem. But, by the fourth quarter of second grade, my son was less than enthusiastic about school in general and was bringing home some poor grades that did not match up with his abilities or his previous love of education.

After several inquiries, we enlisted the help of one of his team teachers. From my son's point of view, this teacher was less than encouraging in her tone of voice and words when dealing with my son. After enforcing new accommodations to ensure he was doing his work, he still got a poor grade on a test. He was heartbroken and so was I. When I attempted to talk with the teacher about making the test a learning experience that he could correct or her reteaching the skill, the teacher's response was less than supportive. I was so sad that after being aware of the life lesson we were trying to teach our son (hard work pays off), the teacher's words were again less than encouraging.

By the time my son went to third grade, I was not expecting much support from the teachers. I had heard that his third grade teacher was strict and mean. I was very concerned; however, the first few weeks of school my son came home excited, loving school again. He reported to me that his teacher, Mrs. Able, told him he had very good ideas in front of the entire class. The comments written on his papers and tests all held positive sentiments. I called Mrs. Able a few weeks into the school year and told her how much we appreciated the encouragement she was giving our son. She responded to me with two things that I will always remember:

#1 She was almost speechless. She had never had a parent call to thank her before. Usually parents called to complain, not compliment her teaching style.

#2 She said my son was amazing, and she wished all of her students were more like him. He had original ideas, and was always willing to participate.

Needless to say, my son thrived under the encouragement of this teacher. I will say, not many parents appreciated this teacher. She was strict and scrutinized every detail of the students' work, but she saved my son. She encouraged him and straightened out the poor work habits he picked up under the watch of his second grade teacher who actually discouraged him. Every time I see my son's third grade teacher, I hug her and tell everyone around that she saved my son and made him the responsible student he is today.

To this day my son, now twelve, is back to his pre-second grade love of learning. Just this summer for fun he read a quantum physics book about the space-time continuum.

I was so pleased to hear one of his teachers recently describe my son as a sponge who just soaks up knowledge. Thank you, Mrs. Able, for using your words of life to give joy in learning back to my son.

This might sound a little melodramatic, but I believe pretty strongly that words do have the power of life or death. Just think, God used His words to create life. We are created in His image, so it seems logical to reason that our words can give life as well. I gave you the example of how Mrs. Able's words gave life to my son's attitude about learning and school. The words this teacher said to him gave him confidence and courage to think and again strive to learn more. I think this principle transcends beyond the classroom. The words we say have power – the power to encourage and give life or the power to discourage and bring death to another's spirit.

I encourage you to be a Mrs. Able in the life of your students. Tell your students why they are remarkable. No student should feel that a teacher doesn't like him or her. I challenge you to use your words to give life to your fellow teachers and administrators as well as students. Tell your fellow educators that they are marvelous. No teacher in your building should be speechless when given a compliment like Mrs. Able was when I called to thank her. I dare you to use your life-giving words to build up each person you come in contact with. Be a life-giver. After all, you were created in the image of the ultimate Life-Giver!

WORKSHEETS

for personal reflection or group discussion:

What:

What principle(s) did I learn from the chapter?

So *What*:

How do these principles impact me?

<u>Now *What*</u>:
What action(s) will I take based on these principles?

<u>*What* Happened:</u>
What evidences do I or others see that these principles have impacted me?

CHAPTER 7

The Thought Life We Choose

Finally, brethren, whatever is true, whatever is honorable, whatever is right, whatever is pure, whatever is lovely, whatever is of good repute, if there is any excellence and if anything worthy of praise, dwell on these things...
Philippians 4:8

As Executive Director of *Christian Educators Association International* I process many phone calls from members. Some need simple encouragement; others need legal support of some kind. However, I do receive a growing number of calls from educators who have been treated in what they believe...and I often agree... is an unfair manner. They describe the incident and want fairness restored. They describe how they can no longer tolerate this situation and want it stopped. Often the behavior they describe is that of a poor administrator - one who focuses on control of staff rather than being a servant leader wanting to assist teachers. Educators are looking to us for a legal remedy, and, unfortunately, there often is not one to give. For you see, there is not a law against being a poor leader...it is simply unprofessional or weak and ineffective leadership.

The best advice I can give is to control the self-talk and focus on being the best educator you can be. Self talk is that thing you say to yourself like, "That is not fair and I cannot take it. I should be getting more support and cannot be an effective teacher without it…etc, etc, etc." Focusing on such self-talk can cause a draining of energy and even bring on hopelessness that can derail a great teacher. It can even end up being self-fulfilling prophesy leading to the destruction of a potentially successful career.

Destructive self-talk is not limited to adults. I remember the challenge as a middle school counselor working with young girls who could not get over the negative things other girls said about them. After working with them for awhile, it became evident that the problem was not what others had said, but what they were saying to themselves. It is this stewing over the words of others that gives power to much of the bullying we see in our schools. When students internalize what others say, it empowers the bully. The bullying escalates rather than diminishes.

I would encourage all of us to regularly ponder Philippians 4:8. I have been in the education business for close to a half a century and I can just about guarantee that as this year progresses many of you will be treated unfairly, feel unsupported, and be spoken to in an abusive manner.

As we encounter such challenges, the only thing we can control is how we respond. One choice would be to ponder the injustice, focus on self-talk about how bad things are, brood and grow the anger into rage. Another would be to apply the same level of grace the Lord gives us to our offenders. We can choose to focus on what is pure and good, and on how blessed we are to be employed and able to have a positive impact on the next generation of parents, business leaders, and politicians.

Grace is a key concept to directing how we respond. It certainly helps me to realize that I would be in great peril if the Lord treated me the way I deserved, but instead He applies Grace to me…can we do any less to others who do us wrong in any way? Scripture is clear on the principle of forgiveness; we receive the same level of forgiveness we give, so I assure you, once I grasped that concept, I allowed forgiveness to flow to others, and thus trigger it to flow to me from the Lord. Does it necessarily mean others will flood me with forgiveness when I offend them...NO! I can only control my response and when I ponder too much the unrighteous way they treat me, I can be heading for personal disaster.

Will the righteous response to negative situations come naturally? No. Retaliation comes more naturally, but as ambassadors of Christ we must choose not to respond from our natural, self-centered sin nature. We increase the potential of responding negatively if we focus our self-talk on the injustice. Our negative self-talk can take on the role of a little devil sitting on our shoulders whispering in our ear that we are being treated unfairly and should take it no longer..."get even" is the mantra that gets repeated over and over again until we pull the trigger, figuratively...I hope not literally...but both versions can end badly.

Let's be honest; our ways are not like His Ways. How can our ways become more like His?

Start every day reading His Word.

I never leave my house in the morning without getting into His Word. For the last thirty plus years I have set up a reading schedule that brings me through the Bible from cover to cover once per year. I am starting to think and act differently as I absorb the Truth. I may be tempted to respond inappropriately or at times respond too quickly, but through the power of the Gospel...forgiveness reigns in the Kingdom. On more occasions than I can even count, as I was reading the Word, I would face a similar situation at work that the Lord had prepared me for in my morning devotions. I soon found that reading His Word everyday was not just a habit I was forming, but it was great preparation for the challenges of the day. Those of us in the world of education know that few days pass without some challenges...some easy to resolve, others needing Divine Insight. I have come to view the Bible as an educators' handbook or guide.

Start every day praising Him for Who He is.

I was not blessed with a musical voice that many beg to hear. I thought only doors and cars needed keys, and quite frankly, I cannot discern one note from another…unless it's being passed in class from one student to another. However, I can sing loudly to the Lord when driving alone in my car. The Lord and I both enjoy my volume and sincerity. I found it empowering to worship and praise Him in this way to prepare myself for the challenges that awaited me at school. God is an awesome God and this helps me to remember that. Imagine that the Creator of the universe loves me and longs to spend time with me. He joys over me and inhabits my attempts at praising Him. These concepts are hard for me to imagine and impossible for me to ignore.

Start every day in prayer laying our issues before Him.

No great move in this nation ever started without the prayers of its people. Even when our forefathers were working on writing the Constitution that still guides this great nation, prayer played a major role. On June 28, 1787 Benjamin Franklin stood up at the Constitutional Convention with some insight on how they might overcome the continued bickering over the language in this document. He said, "…I have lived, Sir, a long time, and the longer I live, the more convincing proofs I see of this truth – that God governs in the affairs of men. And if a sparrow cannot fall to the ground without His notice, is it probable that an empire can rise without His aid? We have been assured, Sir, in the Sacred Writings, that 'except the Lord build the House, they labor in vain that build it.' I firmly believe this, and I also believe that without His concurring aid we shall succeed in this political building no better than the builders of Babel…"

Following this inspiring monologue from one of our more liberal forefathers, the Convention started every session in prayer and moved forward toward completion of this powerful Constitution that is often the envy of the world.

We have two great role models in Scripture to follow on how to respond to perceived adversity: Joseph (end of Genesis) and Daniel (Book of Daniel). A focus on their lives would be a great investment of time in the coming months. Both were treated in an unjust manner yet never departed from their position of faith, never retaliated even when justified. Instead they flourished where the Lord had placed them. They became influencers of the culture rather than victims of the culture.

Joseph could have focused his thoughts on how unfairly his brothers had treated him. Imagine how you might feel. They faked his death and sold him into slavery. He could have become an embittered man, but instead using his giftings he rose to power and influence in Egypt. Ultimately when his brothers came to him begging for food in the time of a famine, he had his chance for revenge, yet he applied grace and was reunited with his family. He allowed God to use him to become a man of great influence and save his people.

Look at the life of Daniel. His home land and family were destroyed by an invading army. Not only was he taken as a slave to a foreign nation, but they even took his name and gave him the name of a foreign god. He could have been justified to focus on negative self-talk in his unfair treatment, but he focused on what he could control: his work ethic, gifting, and his faith. He rose to power and influence under several kings and eventually brought an entire nation to his God.

I look at Daniel as the ultimate role model for teachers in our public schools. Like Daniel we are in a foreign culture – one that is contrary to the Biblical worldview. We can justifiably respond in a rebellious manner as Daniel could have. In fact, we have many more rights to do so than the slave Daniel. However, when confronted with pressure to violate his dietary convictions, Daniel simply appealed to leadership and negotiated a compromise. When it came to the uncompromising issues of his faith-he would worship no other god-he would not compromise knowing it may cost him his life. We could well learn from this great Old Testament prophet.

Starting each day in His Word and investing time in praise and prayer, your ways and your words will start becoming more like His. Dwelling on Him and all that is good is a much better investment of our energies than dwelling on all our injustices and negative issues in our lives. Our self-talk can be a source of life if it focuses on His truths rather than the negative behavior of others and our own shortcomings.

This school year and future ones are overflowing with potential and you and I can play a major role in that potential. How we respond to challenges can make all the difference.

Consider that our goal is not to please all those around us, or to be considered politically correct in all we do. Our goal is to impact the culture around us with God's Love and Truth.

When our careers on earth end, we can look forward to the one evaluation that really matters, "Well done, good and faithful servant."

Parental Commentary

In my counseling classes my professors would often refer to the "tapes we play in our minds." These tapes so often become what we believe about our situation and ourselves. As a parent, I see this evident in my children's lives. I'm sure if you are listening for it, you might hear it from your students. When kids are comfortable around an adult they feel cares about them, they often share a few messages from the tapes playing in their heads.

One of the phrases I use with my children when they are struggling with their thought life is to, "take that thought captive." This phrase is nothing I coined, but actually comes from Paul when he writes in II Corinthians 10: 5 (NIV), "We demolish arguments and every pretension that sets itself up against the knowledge of God, and we take captive every thought to make it obedient to Christ." For the purpose of this chapter, let's take a look at the Message version of this verse as well as the context in which it is set. II Corinthians 10:3-6 (MSG):

The world is unprincipled. It's dog-eat-dog out there! The world doesn't fight fair. But we don't live or fight our battles that way—never have and never will. The tools of our trade aren't for marketing or manipulation, but they are for demolishing that entire massively corrupt culture. We use our powerful God-tools for smashing warped philosophies, tearing down barriers erected against the truth of God, fitting every loose thought and emotion and impulse into the structure of life shaped by Christ. Our tools are ready at hand for clearing the ground of every obstruction and building lives of obedience into maturity.

As you practice taking your thoughts captive, I challenge you to encourage your students to do the same. You don't have to announce that you are including a principle from Scripture. Simply identify negative self-talk. Recognizing its destructive influence on mental health, as well as physical health, is the first step to taking the thought captive, and taking away its power. Most likely, some of your students are even starting to believe lies they have been told and are now replaying these lies on their tapes. Calling a lie a lie is a very powerful way to defeat the effect of the lie.

Once you have identified the negative self-talk, as a Christian, you can use the power of the Holy Spirit to take your negative, unproductive thoughts captive. As a teacher, you can encourage your students to replace that negative thinking with uplifting thoughts. At first, it might be difficult to come up with positive thoughts, especially if the negative thoughts the students are replaying are at least partially true. But you have a wealth of positive thoughts to draw from in the Bible, making you a real resource for your students. For example, if a student is replaying the tape, "I am stupid and worthless," you can replace that thought with, "You are fearfully and wonderfully made." Recognize it? It comes from Psalm 139. Without giving a sermon, you can help equip your student with a truth that will destroy the negative thinking that student has been replaying. Powerful! The cool thing is that the Bible is full of powerful words of truth just like this!

As a parent, I would love to know my children's teachers are speaking words of life and encouragement. They get that from so few sources. Unfortunately, if you are playing negative tapes in your head and you are not familiar with the Words of Life in the Bible, you will be ill-equipped to help your students.

So, I challenge you to be in the God's Word on a regular basis. Be familiar with what God says about you and your students so that you have some positive ammunition in the battle of the thoughts. Watch your own tapes to keep them positive. Please be on the lookout for the negative messages playing in the minds of your students, and be bold enough to speak the truth to them about who God has created them to be. He loves them just as much as He loves you. He has placed these children in your care. Be ready and willing to care for them, please.

WORKSHEETS

for personal reflection or group discussion:

<u>What:</u>
What principle(s) did I learn from the chapter?

<u>So *What*</u>:
How do these principles impact me?

Now <u>*What*</u>:
What action(s) will I take based on these principles?

<u>*What*</u> Happened:
What evidences do I or others see that these principles have impacted me?

CHAPTER 8

Trusting in the Lord

*[1]"I love You, O Lord, my strength." [2] The Lord is my rock
and my fortress and my deliverer, My God, my rock, in
whom I take refuge; My shield and the horn of my
salvation, my stronghold. [3] I call upon the Lord, who
is worthy to be praised, And I am saved from my enemies.
Psalm 18:1-3*

I was a new public school superintendent with my legs still a
bit shaky. The reality is that we can read all the books we can get
our hands on and attend all the classes offered to leaders, but none
really prepare us for true leadership of an entire district...the
same can be said for trying to provide leadership for a single
classroom or mentorship for a single child.

I was thrilled when Bob, a fellow believer and community
member in the district, came and met with me in an effort to let
me know he was ready to serve me...he even used words like,
"As a brother in the Lord, I will lay down my life for you!" Those
were powerful words we all long to hear, but rarely do in this *all
about me culture.*

Bob was an avid sports booster. He was always donating time
and energy to address the building and maintenance challenges
we as a district did not have the skilled staff to address or the
funds to outsource. Bob told me he was praying regularly for me
and my leadership of the district. He felt the Lord was telling him

to serve me at a deeper level. He leaned across my desk and asked if running for a position on the school board would be a way to support me. He said he would still continue to work on maintenance problems and stay active with the boosters, while supporting me the same way Aaron supported Moses. He realized that being a superintendent was at times like being at war with many vying for control or trying to accomplish their personal agendas. There were others who simply fought against any visible representation of authority, and in a school system the obvious target was the superintendent. He assured me, "I will stand behind you and hold your arms as Aaron helped hold Moses' arms as together they witnessed Israel's victory over its enemies."

[10] Joshua did as Moses told him, and fought against Amalek; and Moses, Aaron, and Hur went up to the top of the hill. [11] So it came about when Moses held his hand up, that Israel prevailed, and when he let his hand down, Amalek prevailed. [12] But Moses' hands were heavy. Then they took a stone and put it under him, and he sat on it; and Aaron and Hur supported his hands, one on one side and one on the other. Thus his hands were steady until the sun set. [13] So Joshua overwhelmed Amalek and his people with the edge of the sword. Exodus 17:10-13

No one had ever offered to be my Aaron and the concept of someone standing by my side as I served was appealing...as was having a brother in the Lord whom I could trust and share concerns with. I encouraged him to throw his hat in the ring of leadership. As a popular community figure, he was elected as a board member: now one of my bosses.

For seven years he was a fantastic leader, a confidant, and a brother in the Lord. In his eighth year something changed. Two new non-Christian board members got elected to our five member board, and I noticed Bob was spending much time with them, but they were part of the team after all.

Without notice or any cause I could put my finger on, he verbalized at a public board meeting that I was unwilling to cooperate with the board and he was concerned about this...the other two adversarial board members agreed.. I was shocked as there had been no conflicts and never a strained word between any of the three...and certainly not with my loyal Aaron...holder of my arms...brother in the Lord.

The next few years were among the hardest in my educational career. The three board members worked together to run the district in what was clearly the ungodly trinity. They engaged in such unethical and at times illegal activities as meeting secretly with union representatives to ask what they needed in their next contract; offering to take teachers' requests for teaching and room assignments; interviewing vendors to discuss possible contract deals with the district. This kind of behavior uncovered later ran rampant. They apparently would meet privately in outside meetings to plan their own agendas as I was often blind-sided at our board meetings. When I thought the board business was finished, one of them would add another item I had no idea was coming....with three votes out of five, they became a powerful force of what I believed to be evil.

I was devastated. Up to this time the district had run smoothly. The schooling environment was positive and the business of running a district was by all standards in a good place.

The new board members apparently thought this was their chance to run a school district. They didn't know or care that by state law this was not their role... I could almost understand how their egos had run amuck, but Bob's betrayal took the wind out of my sails. To a much lesser degree...of course...I could almost understand some of the emotions Jesus must have felt when Judas betrayed him for a few pieces of silver. The Judas analogy was driven home when I later learned that the one controlling board member had actually encouraged Bob's betrayal with a major donation to a church project Bob was heading up: his 30 pieces of silver. I was deflated and struggled with how to respond. Bob no longer communicated with me in any manner. It occurred to me that I should still treat him like a brother in the Lord so I went to his house and asked to meet face to face. I asked if I had offended him in some way and was blessed to find I had not, but went on to ask why he no longer supported me, but rather made every effort to undercut my leadership. His honesty and answer did not heal my hurt, but helped me understand. Bob explained, "I reached a leadership position in this community I had only dreamed of. You will be moving on and I simply wanted to stay on the team that would be taking over." I appreciated the honesty, but realized I had not only lost a political supporter, but someone I had counted as a friend.

I found great comfort in the reality that the Lord was my rock and my deliverer. Jesus modeled for us the importance of having a team of believers surrounding us as he depended on his disciples with whom much was accomplished. However, those relationships were not as dependable as the relationship with his Father. Although the disciples eventually were willing to lay down their lives for him, many denied him along the way, failed him at times, and one even outright betrayed him.

It was a great teaching moment for me. It is the Lord only who never changes and will never forsake me. I will not be abandoned by the Lord, but I can never put that level of uncompromised trust in another human being who like me will always fall short.

I hear regularly from educators across the nation who are frustrated and at times ready to give up on a career in which they planned to invest their lives. They look at the plethora of challenges they are facing and see dwindling hope. They are facing an avalanche of challenges: weak administrators, false allegations, unions out of control, parents giving up on their children, continued deterioration of the family unit, friends and even family members that abandon them, sexualization of everything and tolerance of all expressions as normal, pressure to teach to tests, frustrations with working environments, unjust evaluations, gossip in the workplace, fear of being open about faith issues, antagonistic attitudes toward Christianity and tolerance of all other worldviews, negative influences from the federal government, and the list goes on.

I will have to admit that spiritual darkness seems to be spreading across the nation and seeping into the institution that reflects the culture: public schools.

As followers of Jesus, this could be a good thing! That was not a misprint. We are finding that the darker the schooling environments, the more open students, parents, and staff are to things of the Lord. As people are desperate for things of the Lord, the environment is ripe for the revival many of us hunger and pray for.

We hear from missionaries in third world nations that people are coming to the Lord in numbers like never before. In these environments permeated with darkness there is no hope other than reliance on the Lord:

Africa – In 1900 it is estimated there were about 12 million Christians, but today more than 400 million. It is actually the most Christianized continent in the world.

China - It is the fastest growing church in history. In 1950 there were estimated to be 1 to 4 million believers, but today over 100 million believers with 28,000 souls saved a day.

India – It is the second fastest growing church in the world with almost a tripling in size since 1985.

Mongolia – In 1985 there were NO known Christians, but today more than 40,000 believers with over 400 congregations.

Some Latin American countries today are a majority Christian with countries such as Brazil and Argentina sending their own missionaries around the world.

(AIMS: Accelerating International Missions Strategies, 2012)

The Lord is clearly on the move around the globe as more Muslims have come to faith in Jesus Christ in the last twenty years than in all previous centuries COMBINED!

Although a more "fleshly" response to challenges is tempting, the results are quite disappointing. We must stick by the Truth as God sees it, not as others see it. I am reminded of the great role model Daniel was in the Old Testament; even at the risk of death in a lions' den, he did not compromise and the Lord protected him.

He obviously did not know for sure that the Lord would save him, but he did not compromise. Keep in mind, all Daniel had to do was stop praying to the Lord for a time and all would be well with him. He could return to his successful career, and life would be normal again.

When Daniel's friends', Shadrach, Meshach, and Abed-nego, were threatened to be thrown into a furnace if they did not abandon God, they refused. King Nebuchadnezzar said even their god could not save them. They responded,

"...our God whom we serve is able to deliver us from the furnace of blazing fire; ...But even if He does not, let it be known to you, O king, that we are not going to serve your gods or worship the golden image that you have set up."
(Daniel 3: 17-18)

We do not face lions or fire, but often succumb to other pressures rather than taking a stand for our faith. Certainly in times of challenges we need to turn to family, fellow believers, our church leaders, and professional support agencies like CEAI. But we must remember, the only source of support that will never forsake us and will be with us through this life and the next is our Godly Trinity: Father, Son, and Holy Spirit. They will never leave us or forsake us, they will never betray us. They are on our side, and with them on our side, we can rest in a peace that far overpowers whatever challenges come against us. We do not need to rely on our own strengths and gifts. We do not even need to have a full understanding of our current situation: how we got there or how we will escape. Since every day of our life was written out before were even born, we can rest in the knowledge that our challenges did not come as a surprise to our Lord. As His children He loves us even more that we love our children or even ourselves.

[13] For You formed my inward parts; You wove me in my mother's womb. [14] I will give thanks to You, for I am fearfully and wonderfully made; Wonderful are Your works, And my soul knows it very well. [15] My frame was not hidden from You, When I was made in secret, And skillfully wrought in the depths of the earth; [16] Your eyes have seen my unformed substance; And in Your book were all written The days that were ordained for me, When as yet there was not one of them. **Psalm 139:13-16**

Let go of the need to understand, control, or fix the overwhelming challenges you may be facing or may encounter in the future. I am not suggesting you ignore them or pretend they do not exist. I am, however, encouraging you to let go and turn all over to the King of Kings and Lord of Lords....Jesus!

Parental Commentary

Trusting in the Lord... How many times a mother has to do this to get through the day, I cannot tell you. Let's get real. This chapter is about betrayal. The author was terribly wronged by someone he trusted and came to see as a friend. We all face this at some point in our lives. If you haven't yet, I can guarantee you will: a friend, a co-worker, a boss, a neighbor, a child, or a spouse. The true measure of a man (or woman) is how we deal with this betrayal.

I remember when my two-year-old son told me he wanted to throw me in the garbage and never have me come back. I was devastated! I had heard about the horrors of raising a teen, but I never expected to be hurt so deeply by my little first-born while he was still a baby. I had given up everything for this little man: my career and my dignity (dirty diapers and nursing – need I say more?). I deserved to be angry and hurt.

You may have been hurt deeply and caught unaware, just like I was and the author was in his situation. You deserve to be angry and upset. I am agreeing with you. You have been wronged in a terrible betrayal. Let me share with you the secrets I have learned in listening to my Lord and others who love Him when dealing with the ramifications of betrayal.

Who are you? Do you know? I came to realize that I am more than my career, my role as mother, my title in church, and my role in my community. I am God's child. He loves me more than anyone could ever love me, including my spouse, my child, my parents, and my best friend. How do I know this? His Word tells me. I am a dwelling place for the Holy Spirit (Ephesians 2:22), I am a masterpiece (Ephesians 2:10), I am royalty (1 Peter 2:9), I am adopted (Ephesians 1:5), and I am loved (John 3:16). The list of who I am to Christ goes on and on. The cool thing is that you also are all of these things to Him. Once you know who you are, the betrayal loses some of its power. I know this to be true from personal experience.

Bask in His love for you and what He has done for you.

¹⁴This is the reason I kneel in the presence of the Father ¹⁵from whom all the family in heaven and on earth receives its name. ¹⁶ I'm asking God to give you a gift from the wealth of his glory. I pray that he would give you inner strength and power through his Spirit. ¹⁷ Then Christ will live in you through faith. I also pray that love may be the ground into which you sink your roots and on which you have your foundation. ¹⁸ This way, with all of God's people you will be able to understand how wide, long, high, and deep his love is. ¹⁹ You will know Christ's love, which goes far beyond any knowledge. I am praying this so that you may be completely filled with God. Ephesians 3:14-19 GWT

I like this translation because it shows what can happen when we rest in God's presence. We understand and actually FEEL His love for us - a love that is deep, wide, long, and high. It is bigger and stronger than anything we can physically comprehend. If we are plugged in to our God, we can be completely filled with Him and this crazy love! That is truly awesome!

When we are betrayed, we tend to feel a lot of emotions, but most are not love. Anger, bitterness, frustration, and many others seem to rear their ugly heads. Many of our betrayers deserve to receive the wrath of these emotions. The really amazing thing is that we don't have to live with these emotions forever. This passage shows what God can do in our hearts and minds when we come to Him broken and honest, full of these awful-feeling emotions. Yeah God!

Let Him work healing in your heart.

Ephesians 3 goes on to say in verses 20 and 21

²⁰"Glory belongs to God, whose power is at work in us. By this power he can do infinitely more than we can ask or

imagine. [21] *Glory belongs to God in the church and in Christ Jesus for all time and eternity! Amen."*

Our God can heal all sorts of hurts in our hearts. He can do more than we ask or imagine. Do you believe that? Do you trust Him? This is the crux of this chapter. Words are easy to say, "God is good. He can do anything." But actually giving your hurting heart to Him and letting Him take your burden is a completely different experience.

I'm not suggesting that there are no consequences for betrayal, because there are. I am not suggesting that you trust the betrayers, because they may not ever be trust-worthy. However, I can confidently say that you do not need to live in despair and pain. God can deliver you from the pain in your heart resulting from the betrayal.

In addition to the healing of your heart, God can even heal relationships that have been destroyed by betrayal. He can restore family ties. He can restore friendships. He can restore working partnerships. He can even restore marriages that have been blown apart by sin and betrayal.

I encourage you to truly trust in the Lord with ALL your heart, not just the flowers and rainbows part. Give Him your hurts and betrayals. He can handle it! He can heal you from it. Trust Him.

Proverbs 3:5 God's Word Translation

"Trust the Lord with all your heart, and do not rely on your own understanding."

WORKSHEETS

for personal reflection or group discussion:

What:
What principle(s) did I learn from the chapter?

So *What*:
How do these principles impact me?

Now *What*:
What action(s) will I take based on these principles?

What Happened:
What evidences do I or others see that these principles have impacted me?

CHAPTER 9

Bullying

³Now if we put the bits into the horses' mouths so that they will obey us, we direct their entire body as well. ⁴ Look at the ships also, though they are so great and are driven by strong winds, are still directed by a very small rudder wherever the inclination of the pilot desires. ⁵ So also the tongue is a small part of the body, and yet it boasts of great things. See how great a forest is set aflame by such a small fire! ⁶ And the tongue is a fire, the very world of iniquity; the tongue is set among our members as that which defiles the entire body, and sets on fire the course of our life, and is set on fire by hell. ⁷ For every species of beasts and birds, of reptiles and creatures of the sea, is tamed and has been tamed by the human race. ⁸ But no one can tame the tongue; it is a restless evil and full of deadly poison. ⁹ With it we bless our Lord and Father, and with it we curse men, who have been made in the likeness of God; ¹⁰ from the same mouth come both blessing and cursing. My brethren, these things ought not to be this way. ¹¹ Does a fountain send out from the same opening both fresh and bitter water? ¹² Can a fig tree, my brethren, produce olives, or a vine produce figs? Nor can salt water produce fresh. James 3:3-12

I was meeting with Jonny's mom after another incident of bullying in the high school where I had served as principal. As I shared my concern with mom, she broke down and cried admitting she too was being bullied by her son. A pattern we had seen at school was magnified at home.

I would like to say that with a little encouragement from me, Jonny repented and became a positive school citizen and the ideal son. The pattern of abuse was difficult to break, but when working with a powerful team: parent, counselor, administrator, and local pastor, we made great strides that school year.

Not surprisingly, once we broke through the hard shell Jonny outwardly displayed, we discovered he was a hurting young man. He was angry that his father had abandoned him and, from his perspective, his mother did not love him enough to set boundaries. From her perspective, she set no boundaries out of fear to anger him more.

Bullying has many causes: anger, lack of self-confidence, defense mechanism, frustration, and the list can continue. Just as causes can vary, so can the cure. Regardless of the cause, bullying of any kind cannot be ignored.

Bullying continues to arise in schools across the nation as a major issue; a force that brings discouragement, fear, and often disrupts the educational process itself.

HOW DO WE STOP THE BULLYING?

Step one: We need to be sure we are not using words that threaten or put down our charges or peers; make sure all our words are seasoned with grace. We all need to view and treat those around us as ones who are created in the image of God even when they are not acting like it.

Why would step one focus on us instead of others?

First of all, if we want to impact those around us, we must role model the behavior we want to see in others. Bullies are not always the students, but sometimes take the form of those in charge.

I still shudder when I think about the principal who had a fish tank filled with piranhas and would drop in live fish to be devoured in front of elementary students he wanted to intimidate in the discipline process. Then there was the teacher who grabbed a Bible out of the hands of a student in the hallway, smacked him across the chest with it, telling him never to bring that book to this public school again because it violated the separation of church and state!

The remembrance that breaks my heart the most was the middle school teacher who got so frustrated with a school bully, he shoved him up against a locker, lifted him off the ground by his collar, and yelled at him nose to nose, goading him to respond physically. That one breaks my heart because that young beginning teacher was me. Later that day, I got him out of study hall and apologized and asked his forgiveness. How could I expect him to stop intimidating students via my intimidation of him?

Step two: We need to make sure we do everything in our power to stop others from bullying. Far too often open bullying is simply ignored and allowed to grow in negative impact.

As an educator with so many responsibilities on our plates, it is often tempting to ignore the bullying we see around us. The problem is that the carnage left behind by bullies often defeats our primary goal of educating our charges. Sticking our heads in the sand only exacerbates the problems with bullying.

Many districts have clear zero tolerance bullying policies in place, but often ignore them, enforce them sporadically, or use bullying tactics to drive home the intolerance of bullying. We don't want to be a part of this dysfunctional system.

Step three: We need to make sure the school has clear and realistic policies and discipline in place to counter bullying. Often, the usual verbal and physical bullying techniques are covered well in school policies, but many bullies are resorting to using technology as a bullying platform: cyber-bullying. It is imperative that school policies are updated to incorporate cyber-bullying as its presence continues to rise.

Below is some insight on cyber-bullying from CEAI Director of Legal Services La Rae G. Munk, Esq.:

Cyber-bullying most commonly occurs off-campus, yet frequently disrupts and interferes with the education of students. The disciplining of students for cyber-bullying raises unique issues for school leaders, parents and the legal system. Courts and judges are only beginning to consider the ramifications. Across the nation, legislators are struggling with the issue and urging implementation of stricter anti-bullying statutes to address the concerns, particularly as there is more awareness that some of this conduct has led to physical violence and increase in teen suicides.

Following are just three examples I personally have had to address regarding cyber-bullying. I cite them here only to raise awareness of the extensiveness of the types of situations being confronted in our schools today. Hopefully, they provide some awareness to allow pro-active development of policies where some have not yet experienced similar situations. The case law references are presented to offer some guidance in the development of policies and practices for classrooms and school-wide policies.

As the case law across the country indicates, the determination of discipline that can be imposed often revolves around whether the cyber-bullying caused a "substantial disruption or substantial interference" with the educational programs or school safety.

<u>Case 1</u>: Middle school students were not allowed to have telecommunication devices on the school premises. If a child brought a cell phone or similar communication device to school, the item had to be placed in the office and picked up at the end of the school day. On this day within five minutes of dismissal, a complete riot of more than thirty students from two different middle schools located near each other broke out between the two schools because of text messages that flew back and forth between students of the schools. Many of the students remained on the school property as they were using their phones for texting with students at the other school. Those disruptive actions could be addressed under applicable safe school policies, but without a policy addressing disruptions to the education process caused by actions off campus, one of the schools was left with no recourse to discipline students who participated in the cyber-bullying. The other school had the following policy and thus was able to take disciplinary action: *"Bullying" means any written, verbal, or physical act, or any electronic communication, that is intended or that a reasonable person would know is likely to harm one or more pupils either directly or indirectly by doing any of the following: substantially interfering with educational opportunities, benefits, or programs of one or more pupils; or adversely affecting the ability of a pupil to participate in or benefit from the school's educational programs or activities by placing the pupil in reasonable fear of physical harm or by causing substantial emotional distress; or having an actual and substantial detrimental effect on a pupil's physical or mental health; or causing substantial disruption in, or substantial interference with, the orderly operation of the school.*

"At school" means in a classroom, elsewhere on school premises, on a school bus or other school-related vehicle, or at a school-sponsored activity or event whether or not it is held on school premises. "At school" includes conduct using a telecommunications access device or telecommunications service provider that occurs off school premises if the telecommunications access device or the telecommunications service provider is owned by or under the control of the school.

Case 2: Students posed and then posted on *YouTube* a threat of destruction and physical violence to students and staff. The video clip was not created on school property or school equipment. However, as students became aware of the posting, there was considerable disruption to the educational process.

Case 3: A student stole a telecommunication device and proceeded to use the device to send sexually explicit messages to some of the contacts listed on the phone's directory.

Administering cyber-bullying policies effectively has been becoming more difficult without appropriate policies in place in light of such recent decisions as follows.

Layshock v. Hermitage School District, No. 07-4465, __ F3d __, 2011 WL 2305970 (3d Cir. 2011), cited in *Kowalski,* parents sued alleging that they violated their student's First Amendment rights by disciplining him for creating fake internet profile of the principal on popular social networking Internet website, and violated and parents' Fourteenth Amendment substantive due process rights in care and nurturing of their son. The Court of Appeals held that: *student's "entering" district's website to "take" district's photo of principal was not sufficient to forge nexus between school and profile and school district did not have authority to punish student for expressive conduct outside of school that district considered lewd and offensive.*

On the same date, the Third Circuit reached a similar decision in *J.S. v Blue Mountain Sch. Dist., No. 08-4138 (3ʳᵈ Circ. 2011)* affirming a violation of a student's First Amendment free speech rights even though the posting was a parody of a school leader alleging sexually explicit conduct that impacted his life and reputation.

In *T.V. v Smith-Green Comty. Sch. Corp., No. 09-290 (N.D. Ind. Aug. 10, 2011)* 2011 U.S. Dist. LEXIS, two students were disciplined for behavior occurring during summer break and off-campus. The students posed sexually and posted online. The students were suspended based on the school district's policy regarding extracurricular activities. The Court determined the school district had violated the free speech rights of the students and held that the school's policy was "unconstitutionally overbroad and vague."

In *D.J.M. v Hannibal Pub. Sch. Dist., No. 10-1428 (8ᵗʰ Circ. Aug. 2011)*, a student was disciplined by the school district after having sent an instant message on his home computer to the home computer of another student stating that he was going to get a gun and kill certain students. Following the discipline action, the student's parents sued claiming a violation of First Amendment free speech rights. The Court ruled that there was no violation of the student's free speech rights because the speech constituted "unprotected true threats." The Court went on to state that even if his speech was protected under the First Amendment, the school district still was justified in taking discipline action under *Tinker's* substantial disruption standard.

It is proven that school district policies must clearly indicate there is a substantial disruption relationship between the cyber speech activity and the educational process. Whether an individual classroom procedure or a school-wide policy or practice, educators must keep the focus on the extent to which the conduct causes an interruption to instruction.

In summary, we as educators can and must do all we can do to stop the bulling in our schools whether the bully is a student or a fellow staff member; it cannot be tolerated.

<u>Step one</u> : Make sure we are not using words that threaten or put down our charges or peers.

<u>Step two</u> : Make sure we do everything in our power to stop others from bullying.

<u>Step three</u>: Make sure the school has clear and realistic policies and discipline practices in place to counter all forms of bullying.

Parental Commentary

Bullying is quite the hot topic for parents. We worry that either our child will become the victim of the school or neighborhood bully, or that our own sweet child will turn into the bully that the other mothers talk about during mommy outings. Like it or not, educators and parents alike must deal with this issue.

When my middle daughter was in third grade, she began to cry during our bedtime routine. She shared with me that she felt terrible because one little girl in her class was being mean to some of the other kids, forming "clubs" and only letting certain kids into the club. We spent many nights discussing how to deal with the situation. Each night she would come home and report how recess went. One night she was very upset because the bully had singled out another little girl to completely ban from all recess activities and games. My daughter did not like it, but was not sure how to stand up to the bully. All of the other kids were afraid of her. I shared that all of the kids who were silent were only giving the bully power. If they all stood up to her, the bully would lose her control and her power. So my daughter devised a plan, including what she would do and say the next time the bully picked on the little girl. I am so pleased to say that my daughter did it. She stood up for her classmate during the next recess. I was so proud to hear that she could be so strong. I am not sure that at that age I could have been that brave. Well, the bully did not like that my daughter stood up to her, so her focus turned to my daughter, and then spread from the playground at recess into the classroom. Thankfully, my daughter's teacher was paying attention in the classroom and saw the bullying first hand, without my daughter having to tell an adult. The teacher confronted the bully and told my daughter to keep up the good work of standing up for her classmates. The bully has not majorly bullied since this episode years ago.

I learned a few valuable lessons from how my daughter handled this situation. First, I learned that confrontation is not always a bad thing. She used confrontation as a tool to defend someone unable to defend herself. Second, I learned that one does not have to be fearless to be brave. She was nervous but yet she faced the wrath of the bully. She was brave and did what was right. Third, I learned that kids need the adults in their lives to be paying attention and step in when a child needs help. Children do not want to be tattle-tales. My daughter was NOT going to tell the teacher she was under attack, but she did not need to because the teacher was keeping watch over her.

A few years later, I was a volunteer parent chaperone for my son's team trip to camp for a few days. I was shocked at the behavior of a few of the moms. They picked one of the moms to make fun of and exclude from their social chats. I was uncomfortable, but I hate confrontation. It literally makes me sick to my stomach to think that I will have unfriendly words with someone. After being privy to more than one mean chat session with these adult bullies, I thought of my daughter who in third grade stood up for her classmate. I realized that if my daughter could do it, I could too. I am pleased to say that my little girl inspired me to stand up for the mom and ask the other moms to grant her some grace and be kind to her even if she was a little different from them. These moms looked at me like I was crazy. I am sure when I left the room they made fun of me as well, but I took their power away when I sat and chatted with the excluded mom for the remainder of the trip. The author referred to the fact that sometimes adults are just as cruel as child bullies. This is very true.

I share these stories with you because I hope to encourage you. You too can follow the example of a little eight-year-old girl who took a stand on a playground in a small elementary school. You too can use confrontation as a tool to defend your students who are unable to defend themselves. You can pay attention and step in when a child needs help. We parents trust that you are keeping watch over our babies. Every child needs a teacher who cares enough to help keep the school a safe place. Finally, I challenge you to watch out for adult bullies in your school. Often confronting adult bullies is more difficult than child bullies, but you can be brave.

Maybe you could pray that God would reveal any bullies in your school and give you the courage to step out and boldly defend those who are unable to defend themselves. The Holy Spirit will give you the words to say if you ask. You can have courage when you are standing for what is right. With the full armor of God, you can stand firm against anything, even a bully.

WORKSHEETS

for personal reflection or group discussion:

<u>What:</u>
What principle(s) did I learn from the chapter?

<u>So *What*</u>:
How do these principles impact me?

<u>Now *What*</u>:

What action(s) will I take based on these principles?

<u>*What* Happened</u>:

What evidences do I or others see that these principles have impacted me?

CHAPTER 10

Reaching Out
to
Troubled Students

But whoever causes one of these little ones who believe in Me to stumble, it would be better for him if a millstone were hung around his neck, and he were thrown into the sea. Mark 9:42

I remember a middle school student named Todd. Todd was one of those *throw away children.* He was a student not interested in school. His parents did not seem interested in him, and educators were pleased when he did not show up at school. Todd seemed to be an irritant to all. When he missed school, the teachers would hustle to get him caught up. They would hustle to get him caught up; they would hustle, but he could care less. Many teachers gave up, put him in the back of class facing the wall, and ignored him as long as he slept quietly or read his comic books.

Every time there was what appeared to be a juvenile crime in the community, the Sheriff's Department would show up at school to question Todd as he became the community's number one suspect or scapegoat even if not responsible...though many times he was.

I often wonder if I and others on the staff could have done more to support Todd and help him from continuing to stumble. I am unable to forget him as he still shows up on the front page of our local newspaper on occasion. Todd is sitting on death row waiting to be put to death for taking part in the killing of a police informant involved in a drug case many years ago. Todd...even the state sees him as a *throw away kid*...is now an adult with a limited future. He was a throw *away boy* who has become a throw *away man*.

Then there was Steve, an unusual child who did not fit into the schooling culture. Steve was a loner who attached himself to me as his counselor. He was in my office often and even found my phone number and often called me at home. Unusual things started happening in his neighborhood. Barns and garages within walking distance of his home started mysteriously catching on fire.

Then we had a fire set in the school which brought the police to our school wondering if there was a connection...fires continued. I became convinced that Steve was involved and invested time with his parents wanting to get him help before more than property was lost. I asked them if they had to sleep with one eye open wondering if their house was the next target of arson, possibly from within. As often happens, his parents were in denial...until one day a fire was started in their basement. Someone using a blow torch in the basement set the flooring of their bedroom on fire. It was then the denial stopped!

Steve was a small success story as the school in tandem with the parents got him into treatment, and he now is a productive adult in part because we did not count him as a *throw away child*.

Jesus clearly put children in the correct perspective when he talked of children being a priority in His Kingdom and warned others not to cause them to stumble.

We would not be in education if children were not our priority, and we would not purposely cause these children to stumble; however, it is far too easy to focus on the lovable children and ignore or reject the unlovable ones. When we do this, we are not playing a role in stopping them from stumbling – guilt by omission.

WE PLANT SEEDS THAT MAY ULTIMATELY LEAD OUR STUDENTS INTO A PERSONAL RELATIONSHIP WITH THE KING OF KINGS.

Watching and listening to us may be the closest some of our charges get to learning about Jesus; we might be "Jesus with skin on" for them. We certainly are not solely responsible for bringing all our students into relationship with the Lord; that is the job of the Holy Spirit in partnership with the Body of Christ. However, we may be the last caring person between the *throw away child* and a destructive lifestyle that can do unimaginable harm to our culture. We may be one of the last chances to protect future victims from harm or even death.

The job of an educator is not easy, but the potential impact on our culture is powerful. We often talk of the spiritual impact we have on individual students as important…and it is, but education makes a measureable impact culturally as well.

It is easy to feel like a victim of our culture rather than a positive contributor. Often the negative economy, this generation's lack of work ethic, the rise in unlawful behavior, and the deterioration of respect for authority seem overwhelming and we may want to whine, complain, and give up.

The great news is that we are in a position to change this culture one student at a time. Consider investing more of yourself in one or several of the students in your sphere of influence headed toward school failure; your encouragement and support can impact our culture dramatically.

Just one year of increase in the average years of schooling completed correlates with the following average reduction:

Violent crime by 30%,

Motor vehicle theft by 20%,

Arson by 13%,

Buglary & larceny by 6%.

Lochner, L., & Moretti, E. (2004). The effect of education on crime: Evidence from prison inmates, arrests and self-reports. *American Economic Review, 94*(1), 155-189.

WE IMPROVE OUR SAFETY BY SUCCESSFUL EDUCATIONAL EFFORTS.

High school completion alone could have almost unimaginable financial impact:

A one percent increase in high school completion rates for all men age 20-60 would save the United States more than $1.4 billion per year in reduced costs from crime incurred by victims and society at-large.

A five percent increase in male high school graduation rates would produce an annual savings of more than $18.5 billion in crime-related expenses - coupled with annual earnings of those who graduated, the U.S. would receive over $19.7 billion in benefits.

It is a known fact that increasing graduation rates alone will reduce crime and increase earnings significantly. The facts below measure the impact of only a 5% increase in male graduation rates:

Type of Crime	Estimated Decrease in Incidents
Assault	59,160
Burglary	17,256
Larceny	37,334
Motor vehicle theft	31,301
Murder	1,275

Rape 3,816

Robbery 1,509

(Based on national estimates from the *2009 FBI Uniform Crime Report*)

WE IMPROVE OUR ECONOMY BY SUCCESSFUL EDUCATIONAL EFFORTS.

Economically we cannot afford to have less than a stellar education system. Nationally we spend over $12,700 a year to educate a student while we spend over $28,700 annually per inmate with a staggering over $74 billion spent on incarceration nationally.

So what is the moral of this reality? We must all invest our creative efforts to support every student that crosses our path and lead them toward schooling success…we cannot afford to do less. Sometimes letting a student know we care can make the difference between success and failure. Amping up our volume of encouraging words can be explosively powerful. Sometimes we have to search for something positive to say or do for a child, but we must search, find, and respond positively for these future citizens in our culture. Once these students leave our classroom or even our schools, they will become fully functional adults or less; they do not go away even if parents and/or schools *throw them away.*

Each child we invest in was created in the image of God…even when they do not act like it…and each one matters to the Lord. Therefore they should matter to us. As followers of Jesus, we must do all we can to support those students who currently are less than successful in our schooling culture. Many are on the edge of stumbling out of our influence.

His creations matter to Him, so they should matter to us.

TOGETHER WE CAN MAKE A DIFFERENCE ONE STUDENT AT A TIME!

Note: The data referred to in this chapter was collected by the Kentucky Department of Juvenile Justice.

Parental Commentary

I will confess something to you, teachers. There are times when we parents are exhausted and have nothing left to give our kids. We feel overwhelmed and often have no idea how to handle certain issues and situations.

Basically, each of us parents has a "parent tool bag" of sorts. When we find ourselves in need of a tool while parenting, we reach into our tool bag and use what we find. We obtain our tools from a variety of places, but most parents are using the tools they saw their parent use – even the tools they swore they would never use. Parents often find themselves saying things like, "I sound just like my mother/father."

Some parents had excellent role models in their childhood, and their tool bag is full of very effective and useful tools. Some parents read books, attend seminars, and take classes at their churches to gain even more tools for their bag. Each resource to which they expose themselves adds a variety of tools to use when dealing with the multitude of issues and personalities of their children.

Other parents do not have many effective tools in their bags. These parents often were reared in dysfunctional families, and they rarely are even aware of the resources available to them to increase the volume of effective tools in their parent tool bag.

Often, troubled students are living with parents who are ill-equipped to deal with a particular situation, issue, or difficulty. Other times, the personality of one child is so different from a sibling that the tools that effectively helped one child do not work at all for the other. Without a variety of tools, many kids are left unaided in dealing with difficult situations or the fall out of bad decision-making.

Your job can be so much more important than imparting knowledge to your students. You may be able to help the tired, lost parents who are overwhelmed and out of options to help their child. The troubled student in your classroom needs the wisdom and support you can offer. You may be the one person who steps up in the life of a struggling child. You may be "Jesus with skin on" to a student who is being beaten down by the world. You may be able to provide a lifeline to an entire family.

I have another confession. Even parents with well-stocked parent tool bags feel at a loss at one time or another while dealing with their children. Parenting is the most difficult job I have ever had, and the challenges each of my children faced have required many different tools. Every parent needs to feel that someone else is there to help and support a struggling child. I can testify that when I have a child going through a struggle, a caring teacher in my child's corner is such a comfort to me and a help to my child.

Are you prepared to reach out to a troubled student? Are you willing to actually do it?

WORKSHEETS
for personal reflection or group discussion:

<u>What:</u>
What principle(s) did I learn from the chapter?

<u>So *What*:</u>
How do these principles impact me?

Now *What*:
What action(s) will I take based on these principles?

What Happened:
What evidences do I or others see that these principles have impacted me?

Finn Laursen

CHAPTER 11

Sexual Orientation Issues

^{24}Therefore God gave them over in the lusts of their hearts to impurity, so that their bodies would be dishonored among them. ^{25}For they exchanged the truth of God for a lie, and worshiped and served the creature rather than the Creator, who is blessed forever. Amen. ^{26}For this reason God gave them over to degrading passions; for their women exchanged the natural function for that which is unnatural, ^{27}and in the same way also the men abandoned the natural function of the woman and burned in their desire toward one another, men with men committing indecent acts and receiving in their own persons the due penalty of their error. Romans 1:24-27

I was presenting at a three-day teachers' seminar for Christian educators working in public schools. The issue of teachers unions came up on day-two as did discussions of why some Christian educators refuse to join the union and instead join *Christian Educators Association International* as an alternative.

I went on to explain that some do not want to support the agendas of the unions like the support of liberal political candidates, the support of abortion, and the promotion of the gay agenda to name a few. The latter two are often the focus of teachers who become religious objectors in forced union states and thus end up giving no money to the unions, not even fair share or agency fees. However, in some cases the unions insist they give donations to an agreed upon charity as an alternative...legal in all forced union states.

I was shocked when one of the participants did not return for day-three, but instead sent a scathing email claiming I had taken a homophobic position contrary to what he believes Christianity espouses. His email said:

"Apparently, I am one of those dreaded liberals who has a wide tolerance for all people and beliefs. One of my core beliefs is that when Jesus asked us to love one another he meant exactly that. Love one another just as they are. Any race, national origin, creed, belief system, sexual preference, handicap, etc. just love them."

I contacted him and apologized for offending him and wanted to meet and discuss the issues, which he refused to do.

Had he allowed such a meeting and discussion, I would have explained that I agree that we should love all regardless of their belief system, creed, sexual preference, etc, but it does not mean we must embrace, endorse, or promote their faith or lifestyle.

[13]Enter through the narrow gate; for the gate is wide and the way is broad that leads to destruction, and there are many who enter through it. [14] For the gate is small and the way is narrow that leads to life, and there are few who find it. Matthew 7:13-14

My understanding is that the *Great Commandment* calls us to love God and others, and the *Great Commission* calls us to tell all the Truth about our Lord and spread the Gospel to all. Neither one calls us to embrace and endorse all beliefs or lifestyles.

I recently got a call from a member concerned with an in-service she just attended within her district. It was promoted as an anti-bullying in-service, but was clearly focused on the issue of sexual orientation. During the program the superintendent clarified that if any of the students verbalized or exhibited behavior or dress different from the stereotypical heterosexual orientation, the staff would be required to support and endorse. Any other response would be considered bullying and sexual harassment and would result in termination.

Believing such a lifestyle to be contrary to Biblical mandates, she was devastated and wanted counsel on how to respond.

I suggested looking at the Prophet Daniel as a role model. He lived, succeeded, and prospered in a culture foreign to him and not honoring to his God. Without compromising his convictions, he served several kings and continued to grow in influence. I suggested she show love and grace to all her students and could clearly do that without endorsing lifestyle decisions contrary to her faith. If students ask her questions or advice, I suggested she be honest as the courts are still defending the free speech rights of public school teachers...in most cases. Could being honest with students when asked about personal questions lead to discipline and loss of a job? Perhaps, but if sensitive to what the Lord is leading, I believe at times we must take a few risks to defend the Truth. Daniel stayed true to the Lord and would pray to no other...there was a cost that he was willing to pay not knowing if the Lord would protect him or not. Notice that he did not stand in the public square to challenge the king's order to pray only to him, but privately stayed true to his Lord and the Lord did protect him when he was thrown into the lion's den for disobeying the king's order.

There may come a day when those who are followers of Jesus are not welcome in the public sector, but today they are. Today we can have a transformational impact on the culture if we see our roles as agents of the Lord.

There is no doubt that the homosexual agenda abounds within the schooling community. This pervasive push to accept the same sex attraction as normal is what many in our modern culture embrace as being politically correct, and any other opinion is dismissed as hateful and cruel. A lifestyle estimated to be chosen by about two percent of our population has become the focus of the anti-bullying movement and has been incorporated into all facets of the media. This agenda twists medical facts and Biblical truth, trying to convince all that such sexual behavior is normal and should be not only be embraced, but celebrated. Curriculum is even surfacing that tries to prove such behavior is not only natural, but an obvious outcome of evolution.

School officials are being increasingly pressured by pro-homosexual organizations to integrate homosexual education into school curricula. These organizations recommend promoting homosexuality as a normal, immutable trait that should be validated during childhood, as early as kindergarten. These organizations also condemn all efforts to provide reparative therapy to gender confused students, advocating the creation of student groups that affirm homosexual attractions and behaviors instead.

Across the nation some Christian students are standing on Biblical Truth to counteract this effort and at times have challenged educators' efforts to maintain order. Some schools have actually punished students who have offered a differing opinion on the issue of same sex attraction than the politically correct position promotes. In an effort to help schools deal with this potentially explosive conflict of opinion, I was invited to represent the Christian view on the issue at a convention of the *National School Board Association*. Joining me on the stage was the head of the *Gay, Lesbian, & Straight Education Network* (GLSEN) along with two attorneys. The issue at hand was whether students had the right to express a stand on Biblical Truth that might offend some who embrace or practice an alternative lifestyle.

I saw emotions escalate when I suggested that all wanted a safe environment for everyone, but I saw the conflict over the fact that many educational anti-bullying efforts tried to reduce the bullying by promoting homosexual behavior and lifestyle as normative. The head of GLSEN angrily got in my face and yelled, "We are normal; we are here; get used to it Laursen!"

By the time the filled-to-capacity gathering ended, I think most agreed that students did have a right to express their First Amendment protected religious convictions and could not be forced to relinquish those to spare hurt feeling of those opposed. However, I suggested that students could express those beliefs in a loving and compassionate manner, realizing that not all in the public arena may agree with their beliefs.

The *CEAI Membership Service Center* continues to be inundated with requests for Godly responses to such pervasive efforts to capture the minds of our children and staff as well as the student conflicts it elicits. The question arises regularly at our conferences and seminars because it does not seem safe to even discuss the issues at the school level.

All children are precious in the Lord's sight and were created in His image; we must therefore protect them from bullying as well as from the twist that all should accept homosexuality as normal to curtail bullying.

The best response to untruth is obviously truth.

One source of clarity and research based truth on sexual issues was a project of *The American College of Pediatricians.* They developed a great website for educators to refer to when challenged with such issues.

Below is a list of true statements taken from this valuable website: http://factsaboutyouth.com/.

- Homosexuality is not a genetically-determined, unchangeable trait.

- Homosexual attraction is determined by a combination of familial, environmental, social and biological influences. Inheritance of predisposing personality traits may play a role for some. Consequently, homosexual attraction is changeable.

- Most students (over 85%) with same-sex attractions will ultimately adopt a heterosexual orientation if not otherwise encouraged. Most questioning students are experiencing temporary sexual confusion or are involved in experimentation.

- The homosexual lifestyle, especially for males, carries grave health risks.

- Declaring and validating a student's same-sex attraction during the adolescent years is premature and may be personally harmful.

- For many youth, homosexual attraction develops due to negative or traumatic experiences, such as sexual abuse. These students need therapy for the trauma, not affirmation of a "gay identity."

- Sexual reorientation therapy has proven effective for those with unwanted homosexual attractions.

- There is no evidence that pro-homosexual programs, such as on-campus student clubs, ease the health risks or emotional disorders suffered by homosexuals.

- Regardless of an individual's sexual *orientation*, sexual *activity* is a conscious choice.

- It is in the best interest of all students to refrain from any sexual activity until adulthood; most optimally until they enter a life-long faithful marriage.

- The school's responsibility is to provide a safe environment for respectful self-expression for all students. It is not the school's role to diagnose and attempt to treat any student's medical condition, and certainly not the school's role to "affirm" a student's perceived personal sexual orientation.

The Facts about Youth resource can substantiate the above facts and provide other useful resources for educators.

Sexual orientation issues continue to be divisive in our public schools and even within the faith community. As each of us decides how to best deal with these issues at work, at church, and at home, let's remember another truth:

The Excellence of Love

[1]If I speak with the tongues of men and of angels, but do not have love, I have become a noisy gong or a clanging cymbal. [2]If I have the gift of prophecy, and know all mysteries and all knowledge; and if I have all faith, so as to remove mountains, but do not have love, I am nothing. [3]And if I give all my possessions to feed the poor, and if I surrender my body to be burned, but do not have love, it profits me nothing.

[4]Love is patient, love is kind and is not jealous; love does not brag and is not arrogant, [5]does not act unbecomingly; it does not seek its own, is not provoked, does not take into account a wrong suffered, [6]does not rejoice in unrighteousness, but rejoices with the truth; [7]bears all things, believes all things, hopes all things, endures all things. [8]Love never fails; but if there are gifts of prophecy, they will be done away; if there are

tongues, they will cease; if there is knowledge, it will be done away. [9]For we know in part and we prophesy in part; [10]but when the perfect comes, the partial will be done away. [11]When I was a child, I used to speak like a child, think like a child, reason like a child; when I became a man, I did away with childish things. [12]For now we see in a mirror dimly, but then face to face; now I know in part, but then I will know fully just as I also have been fully known. [13]But now faith, hope, love, abide these three; but the greatest of these is love.
I Corinthians 13

Parental Commentary

I was raised to see sexual activity as something wonderful and sacred. I guarded my sexuality until I was married. Still, I save myself for my husband and him alone. I believe God intended for our bodies to be used to glorify God and bless our spouses.

When I was a child, sexuality was not blatantly flaunted and treated as disrespectfully as it is now. This young generation faces a great challenge to behave in opposition to the culture shown on television, in popular music, and in our school halls. I pray for my kids continually, and remind them that their bodies are temples of the Holy Spirit. They will have to stand firm against the frighteningly strong influences of the culture pulling them towards disrespecting their bodies, and away from the purity to which God has called them.

My husband and I teach our children not to be embarrassed of their bodies, because they are fearfully and wonderfully made. They are free to ask us any question without fear that we will be upset with them or that we will embarrass them for asking. We commit to tell them the truth, and if we don't know the answer, we research to find it. For now, they have been very open to our knowledge, trusting that we are telling them the truth. In fact, my oldest son told his younger sister the following analogy:

"Think of all of the advice and information you get about sex from your friends like the sand at a beach. Then picture yourself picking up one grain of sand. That is about how much truth your friends will give you. The rest of the sand on your beach is false. Your friends are stupid. They don't know anything. Ask mom and dad and they will tell you the truth." (He was only 9 when he said this!)

I almost did a flip when I overheard this conversation, because I was so happy. Then I realized most kids are not being told the truth by their parents. Most likely, your students are getting their information from prime time television and the locker room. Their minds are being filled with tons of sand, not truth. They are building their sexual lives on a foundation of sand, which we know is the worst possible material for a foundation.

[24] Therefore everyone who hears these words of Mine and acts on them, may be compared to a wise man who built his house on the rock. [25] And the rain fell, and the floods came, and the winds blew and slammed against that house; and yet it did not fall, for it had been founded on the rock. [26] Everyone who hears these words of Mine and does not act on them, will be like a foolish man who built his house on the sand. [27] The rain fell, and the floods came, and the winds blew and slammed against that house; and it fell—and great was its fall. Matthew 7:24-27

They don't even realize they are setting themselves up for a crumbling sexual life because they are deceived. They see their sin as normal. The scary fact is that sexual sin is a sin against your own body.

¹⁸Flee immorality. Every other sin that a man commits is outside the body, but the immoral man sins against his own body. ¹⁹Or do you not know that your body is a temple of the Holy Spirit who is in you, whom you have from God, and that you are not your own? ²⁰For you have been bought with a price: therefore glorify God in your body. I Corinthians 6:18-20

I have seen the effects of sexual sin in the lives of teens first hand. I started a *Teen MOPS* group at our local crisis pregnancy center where we create a safe, Christ-centered environment for young moms ages thirteen to twenty-one. We encourage and equip these precious young ladies to realize their potential as young women, moms, and leaders. When talking with these young women, I can see the cycle of teen pregnancies in many of their families. I can see the hurt and hopelessness these young ladies and their baby-daddies feel. Most of them, even the Christian girls, never considered abstaining from sex until marriage. That concept is not in their culture. I know girls who experiment with bisexuality to avoid pregnancy because their sexuality is built on a sandy foundation. They have been deceived. The idea of respecting their bodies and their sexuality is completely foreign to them.

This is where those of us chosen to interact with these children get to share Grace, Truth, and Love. At *Teen MOPS* these girls are loved like crazy! We don't judge them or make them feel guilty. We speak the Truth to them: God loves them; God has a plan for them; God has guidelines to make their lives better, including their sex life. Unfortunately, a few of our girls continue making bad choices. We've even had a few return to our group pregnant again. They hear the truth the first time we share it, but they don't really listen. Do we approve of their choices? No, but they come back to *Teen MOPS* to feel God's love and our support. And they are lovingly told again and again about God's love and His plan for them. They learn how to read the Bible, where they hear the Truth yet again. We pray over them and their children. We are examples for them. As *Teen MOPS* leaders, we cannot make decisions for these children, but we can be instruments of Grace, Truth, and Love. We have found that if we demonstrate a different way of living through our examples and give the girls grace when they make a bad choice, they are more open to the Truth. I am very pleased to say that several of our girls do hear and listen to our message. They see the plan the Lord has for them, and they feel His Love and Grace change their lives. At *Teen MOPS* they are getting rocks of truth on which to build a new foundation - rocks that are held together with God's Grace, Truth, and Love.

Likewise, you cannot make decisions for your students, but you can be an instrument of Grace, Truth, and Love. If you demonstrate a different way of living and give your students grace when they make a bad choice, they will most likely be more open to the Truth.

I would like to clarify, grace does NOT include finger pointing, put downs, or eye-rolling (no matter how frustrated you are with the child's choices). If you ever expect your students to be open to the Truth, you need to start with grace. Seeing your students as God does and praying for them will significantly help you show your students His Love. Thankfully, God's Love for us is not dependent on our choices and behavior. His Love for your students is just as strong as His Love for you, so stay connected with the source of His Love, and you won't be able to stop loving your students.

Truth can only be effectively conveyed if you are a living example of the concept. *Do what I say, not what I do* is NOT effective when dealing with sexual integrity. No matter what level you are teaching, you all lead by example. Are you dressing appropriately? Are the words coming out of your mouths promoting purity? If you are single, are you practicing sexual integrity? If you are married, are you being sexually faithful to your spouse? This includes pornography and internet "friendships." You are sinning against yourselves if you are being deceived into believing the sand is a solid foundation.

I send my three children to public schools, and I (along with every other Christian parent whose kids are in public schools) am trusting that they are not being influenced in your classroom to believe that the sand is a safe place to build their sexual foundation. Please be an example of sexual integrity, and shower your students with Grace, Truth, and Love. Moms like me are counting on Christian teachers like you. Our kids are being shoveled enough sand outside of your classroom.

WORKSHEETS
for personal reflection or group discussion:

<u>What:</u>
What principle(s) did I learn from the chapter?

<u>So *What*:</u>
How do these principles impact me?

Now *What*:
What action(s) will I take based on these principles?

What Happened:
What evidences do I or others see that these principles have impacted me?

CHAPTER 12

The Spiritual Realm

The seventy returned with joy, saying, "Lord, even the demons are subject to us in Your name." Luke 10:17

Another week of challenges as a building level administrator seemingly had come to an end as I was organizing myself to head home one Friday afternoon. But first I needed to meet with one of our counselors who had asked to connect after school on a personal matter.

Besides my role as administrator, I also believe the Lord had placed me in the public schools as His representative. I never turn down such a request as I was finding such opportunities often opened the door to talk about faith issues. This was no exception. This counselor, Bart, poured his heart out about his life's challenges including a failed marriage, challenges in a new marriage, and general unhappiness with his life. As the tears welled up, he went on to say that he wanted to experience some level of the joy and peace he saw in me. He had been watching me and noticed that level of peace never seemed to falter regardless of the circumstances.

I could see where this was going, so I settled back and listened. Eventually, I was able to give my testimony and tell him about my source of peace. I told him I could relate to the lack of peace he felt since I had once experienced the same discontent. I admitted that I went through a period earlier in my career that I felt under such pressure that I started out many Mondays vomiting in anticipation of the day's challenges yet unseen. I further shared, as he listened intently, that I had come into a personal relationship with the Lord. I was filled with the Holy Spirit, and my life became transformed. I still had challenges, but my source of peace, joy, and hope became the Lord.

His tears increase as he proclaimed, "That is what I need; that is what I want!"

I prayed him through the sinners prayer and we asked for the infilling of the Holy Spirit. As we said, "Amen," Bart stood up quickly, looked me in the eyes, and said, "Finn, do not trust me; I'm going to hurt you; get out…"

Then something happened that quite frankly I almost hesitate to record as I might doubt the reality of it if I had not experienced it! Bart's facial form shifted as the skin on his face seem to change position, his eyes rolled back in their sockets, and he started animalistic growling in a voice other than his own. He started to come towards me with his hands held in a claw-like fashion.

This was just like a demonic scene from a horror movie, except it was real and here we were alone in a school building with no one around to help me. I remembered his warning not to trust him because he would hurt me…I was almost paralyzed with fear and at a loss on what to do.

I was a fairly new Christian with no training or insight in dealing with the demonic, but I clearly understood that Bart was demon possessed and his attempt to come to faith had awakened the evil one within. His warning to me also confirmed that he knew of its presence, but was not equipped to control it, as it controlled him.

I sort of believed in the reality of a spiritual realm, but had never expected to be thrust into the middle of such a battle. I realized I may be facing death. I remember reading or being told that at the name of Jesus even the demons cower. I remember Jesus' young disciples were shocked that demons were subject to them in the name of Jesus...I remember singing of the power of His Name in church.

I did not have time for a theological study or debate as my once docile friend was reaching toward me with his claw like hands growling with a contorted face. Only the whites of his bloodshot eyes showed.

I held out my hands in a show of authority I did not feel inside and shouted, "Stop in the name of Jesus!" Much to my surprise, he froze in his steps as he continued his menacing growl, but he took the position of a cornered, wounded animal.

I was not equipped nor did I have the confidence to decide my next move, so I called my church and got the number of one of the elders who I had heard was involved in deliverance ministry. When I described what I was in the midst of he calmly, as if this was a normal happening, asked if I could get Bart to the church and he would meet us there. It was help from someone not accusing me of hallucination, so I grabbed the offer and hoped...prayed...that I could even get Bart into my car without being killed in the process.

I started giving him orders always "in Jesus' name" and every time he obeyed. At times Bart would seem to return with his own voice, but only for short intervals.

I got him out to my car, but when I opened the door, he froze telling me his feet felt like they were set in concrete and he was unable to lift them. I reverted to what worked and ordered step by step in Jesus' name till he was in the front seat of my car.

The battle continued all the way to the church. Several times he grabbed the steering wheel trying to wreck the car, but my new power over him in Jesus' name released his grip. At one time he told me my house was on fire and my wife needed to be rescued.

In my limited spiritual understanding I yelled, "Satan you are the father of lies…in Jesus' name be quiet!" Again he obeyed.

I was met in the parking lot by the church elder and after going inside and discussing what had happened, Bart was himself much of the time and agreed to submit to the elder's ministry. During our dialogue Bart shared that he remembered being lonely as a young boy and inviting in this spirit to keep him company. During the initial prayer time, the elder called on every name used for the Lord in Scripture. I was in shock when the demon took over again and praised Satan. I say the demon took over because the voice was clearly not that of my friend. Plus, he had no Biblical background, so he would never even have known the names the demon was proclaiming about Satan.

At the end of the evening, the battle clearly was not over. Several times during our ordeal, Bart asked us to simply call an ambulance and get him medicated as he was a professional with an MA and these things could not be happening. Bart agreed to continue meeting one on one with the elder. I agreed to help him cleanse his office of things not edifying to the Spirit. I called his wife explaining that I had been with Bart at church for prayer and asked her to pick him up.

In the coming weeks I helped him go through items we found in his office at school: skulls of dead animals, wall wreaths made of weaved hair from dead people, symbols of darkness, and a dominance of the color black.

For several weeks I saw great progress and he continued to submit to the deliverance ministry at church as well as my counsel and support at work.

Then it happened. He came to me one day and told me that the last few weeks didn't happen, and I was never to bring it up as he would deny it. He was an educated man who does not believe in that spiritual mumbo jumbo. He no longer talked with me or even gave me eye contact.

As time passed and I moved on to another district, I saw his life spiral downward. He stayed deep in denial as his marriage imploded and he sought relief with sexual escapades that left him empty and void of peace or happiness. He continued to be drawn to the darkness and things dealing with death.

So what has my involvement with deliverance ministry been since this isolated experience? I am grateful to be able to say, very little. However, it has raised my awareness of the spiritual realm; that it is not a throwback to the middle ages, but is real and impacting our lives today. At times I have experienced what I think of as a discerning Spirit, being able to sense that the evil one or one of his followers is around. I have experienced a tightening of the chest and a difficulty in breathing when this occurs. This happened on two occasions when it was discovered that a priest of the church of Satan was in our midst.

This was not a gifting I asked for and am blessed that it has not surfaced often. I must admit I only share this reality with a few believers I trust because I am aware that the reality of the supernatural may not be edifying to non-believers and even to many within the Body of Christ.

However, these experiences have raised my awareness to the truth that the spiritual realm is real and must be dealt with as such:

[11]Put on the full armor of God, so that you will be able to stand firm against the schemes of the devil. [12]For our struggle is not against flesh and blood, but against the rulers, against the powers, against the world forces of this darkness, against the spiritual forces of wickedness in the heavenly places. [13]Therefore, take up the full armor of God, so that you will be able to resist in the evil day, and having done everything, to stand firm. Ephesians 6:11-13

Experiencing this reality has strengthened my prayer life and my reliance on prayer. Prayer is a true communion with the Creator of the Universe, and with it we have been given the power to take dominion over our earthly dwelling places.

As a principal and later as a superintendent of schools, I went through all our buildings before teachers returned from summer vacation and prayed over all the classrooms and hallways and even anointed with oil all the doorways that students would soon be passing through. I prayed protection over the building and all who would soon enter there. I prayed that no spirit other than the Holy Spirit would have dominion over those entering these buildings. This was not a practice I shared with many knowing many would simply dismiss it as foolishness and I could not find it listed within my job description.

How would such a reality impact you and your career as an educator? Do you need to become some kind of fanatic and chase out demons from every corner or person you meet? Probably not!

However, I suggest you take seriously the reality of a spiritual realm realizing that at times you may find yourself under a spiritual attack or oppression of some kind. The only remedy for spiritual attack is to rely on our Lord as your Protector and rely on His Power to see you through.

I have heard testimonies of teachers who began praying over the desks of their students before they arrive in the morning and found a measurable change in student behavior result. Magic? No, but we must remember that we exist in a physical realm, but can be influenced by the spiritual. I'm not suggesting you focus all your energies on spiritual warfare, but you should acknowledge it exists. If you are in relationship with the Lord, you do not need to surrender to spiritual warfare. Acknowledging that the spiritual realm is real can also be encouragement to get prayer coverage from fellow believers. After all, we are the Body of Christ, not the lone rangers of Christ. Together with Jesus we are an unbeatable team.

Let's continue to make a difference... in Jesus' name... AMEN!

Parental Commentary

This chapter could result in several responses from you, the reader. You could think the author is crazy. You could pretend this isn't real and just skim through it. Or you could be freaking out right now. Hopefully, you are not reacting in any of these ways. The intent of this chapter is to draw your attention to the reality of Ephesians 6:10-20.

[10]Finally, be strong in the Lord and in his mighty power. [11]Put on the full armor of God, so that you can take your stand against the devil's schemes. [12]For our struggle is not against flesh and blood, but against the rulers, against the authorities, against the powers of this dark world and against the spiritual forces of evil in the heavenly realms. [13]Therefore put on the full armor of God, so that when the day of evil comes, you may be able to stand your ground, and after you have done everything, to stand. [14]Stand firm then, with the belt of truth buckled around your waist, with the breastplate of righteousness in place, [15]and with your feet fitted with the readiness that comes from the gospel of peace. [16]In addition to all this, take up the shield of faith, with which you can extinguish all the flaming arrows of the evil one. [17]Take the helmet of salvation and the sword of the Spirit, which is the word of God.

[18]And pray in the Spirit on all occasions with all kinds of prayers and requests. With this in mind, be alert and always keep on praying for all the Lord's people. [19]Pray also for me, that whenever I speak, words may be given me so that I will fearlessly make known the mystery of the gospel, [20]for which I

***am an ambassador in chains. Pray that I may declare it
fearlessly, as I should.***

You are a part of God's army to defeat the efforts of the
enemy.

As a parent of three children in public schools, I am keenly
aware of the spiritual battle over the souls of my children. Every
bus ride is a battle. Every time my kids are exposed to ungodly
music is a battle. Every swear word they hear on the playground
is a battle. Every inappropriate book all the other kids are reading
is a battle. Every bully in the neighborhood is a battle.

You get another glimpse into the thoughts of a Christian mom
here. Are you ready? I am counting on you to be praying over my
kids. I am counting on all of the Christians in my kids' schools to
be covering them with the prayers of protection, boldness, and
steadfastness.

Are you ready for this? There are Christian moms all over the
world praying for you as well. I speak from experience. I am a
mom who gathers each Sunday night with a group of other
Christian moms to pray for the employees of our local school
district. We literally pray Scripture over each employee, focusing
on one or two a week. We pray passionately for our kids, the
educators in our district, and their schools. You have a cheering
squad. Did you know that? Not all parents are angry and think
you are the enemy. Some of us are praying for you like crazy. We
are not only counting on you, but we are supporting you against
attacks from the evil one. We are also praying for our little ones.
Please join us in the real battle - not the battle of test scores or
reaching standards – but the spiritual battle for the lives of your
co-workers and your students, our children.

I am a member of a *Moms In Prayer* group. We are all over
the world. You can find out where the *Moms In Prayer* group is
meeting to pray for your school by looking it up on their website
momsinprayer.org.

Also, I encourage you to learn to pray Scripture over your students. A resource I use is *Praying the Scriptures for your Children; Discover How to Pray God's Purpose for Their Lives* by Jodie Berndt. I believe the Word of God is living and active and will NOT return void. This new way of praying over your students might be as transformative to your classroom as it was to my family.

As I write this response, I am praying Ephesians 6:11-18 over you.

" Lord, cloth your precious one with Your full armor so that he can take his stand against the devil's schemes. Help him to stand firm, with the belt of truth buckled around his waist and the breastplate of righteousness in place. Fit his feet with the readiness that comes from the gospel of peace. Give your warrior the shield of faith, with which he can extinguish all the flaming arrows of the evil one. Place the helmet of salvation on his head and the sword of the Spirit, which is Your Word, in his hands. Finally, teach him to pray, and to be alert. " (Taken in part from *Praying the Scriptures for your Children Discover How to Pray God's Purpose for Their Lives* by Jodie Berndt)

May God bless you, educator, as you make a difference for the Lord where He has placed you.

WORKSHEETS

for personal reflection or group discussion:

<u>What</u>:
What principle(s) did I learn from the chapter?

<u>So *What*</u>:
How do these principles impact me?

<u>Now *What*</u>:
What action(s) will I take based on these principles?

<u>*What* Happened</u>:
What evidences do I or others see that these principles have impacted me?

Finn Laursen

Appendix

Christian Educators Association International (*CEAI*) is a non-profit, religious association serving as a membership professional association for Christian educators and support staff in public and private schools. *CEAI* membership consists of teachers, administrators, para-professionals including any person hired by a school district. In addition, they offer associate membership to parents, pastors, school board members, youth leaders and others concerned or interested in the education of our children.

CEAI is the only association providing services including professional liability and job action legal protection specifically for Christians serving in public schools. Many Christians are choosing to join *CEAI* as an alternative to the secular unions who are supporting anti-family agendas.

Check them out at their website today at www.ceai.org where you can find many resources and can become a member. *CEAI* exists to serve!

CEAI is a 501 (c)3 Religious Non-Profit.

Vision:

God's Love and Truth Transforming our Schools.

Mission:

To Encourage, Equip and Empower Educators according to Biblical Principles.

- Proclaim God's Word as the source of wisdom and knowledge

- Portray teaching as a God given calling and ministry

- Promote educational excellence as an expression of Christian commitment

- Preserve our Judeo-Christian heritage and values through education

- Promote the legal rights of Christians in public schools

- Provide a forum on educational issues with a Christian world view

- Partner with churches, parachurch organizations, educational institutions and parents

- Provide resources and benefits for educators including professional liability insurance

MEMBERSHIP BENEFITS

Benefits can be viewed at http://www.ceai.org

PROFESSIONAL LIABILITY INSURANCE

Members receive legal defense and protection for their assets (up to $2,000,000) when faced with a lawsuit related to their profession.

LEGAL AND EDUCATIONAL CONSULTATION

Members have access to an attorney or experienced educator to discuss legal or educational issues related to your employment. Referrals to outside legal services will be made when appropriate.

JOB ACTION PROTECTION

Members receive coverage of legal fees in case of job actions such as demotion, termination or non-renewal. Legal advice and local representation is provided when needed.

STAFF SUPPORT

Staff members are ready to assist you. It only takes a phone call (1-888-798-1124) to get your questions answered or concerns resolved.

BIBLICAL WORLDVIEW VOICE

CEAI voices the needs of Christian educators. We impact the educational community and our culture from a Biblical worldview through publications, news media, personal contacts, etc.

$40,000 TERM-LIFE INSURANCE

New Members may be eligible to receive $40,000 of group term insurance* for two years at no cost. *subject to carrier underwriting approval.

SUPPLEMENTAL INSURANCE PRODUCTS

Members can purchase life insurance, health insurance, dental coverage, auto coverage and a variety of other insurance products at an economical group rate.

DISCOUNT BENEFITS PACKAGE

A discount benefits package available to you and your family. This package includes huge on-line savings, availability to discounts, wellness resources, and even 24/7 access to medical doctors without office fees attached. All this for a low monthly fee.

TEACHERS OF VISION MAGAZINE

Keep abreast of issues affecting Christian educators through *Teachers of Vision*, a national magazine published by *CEAI*.

NEWSLETTERS

Members receive on-line monthly newsletters with informative articles and the latest in education news.

INTERNET RESOURCES

You can interact with attorneys and network with other members online, sign-up to receive daily devotionals, visit our online store and have access to many other valuable resources at ceai.org.

PRAYER NETWORK

Members can call or email (prayer@ceai.org) with prayer requests or to be linked with other members for prayer support. We will assist you to form prayer groups at your school.

LOCAL CHAPTERS AND NETWORKS

A formal chapter or informal network may be established right in your own community. Both enable members to meet regularly with teachers, parents and other Christians who share the same vision and values. Through such interaction, educators are sharpened and become more effective for Christ in the classroom.

LOCAL SEMINARS

Teachers are empowered, equipped and encouraged at local seminars around the country. Educators receive powerful input on how to legally and effectively impact their school culture with their faith. Sharing of successful ideas and creative approaches are an encouragement to all.

MEDICAL/HEALTH CONSULTATIVE SERVICES

Members and family can call 1-866-890-CARE (2273) to receive the support of *Lighthouse with Healthcare Solutions* at no charge. They are a "single-point contact" that provides confidential assistance to those struggling with drug and alcohol addictions, eating disorders, anxiety and stress disorders, sexual addictions, gambling and other life-controlling behaviors.

CREDIT UNION MEMBERSHIP

As a member of *CEAI* you are entitled to participate in a membership service with the *Christian Community Credit Union*. Services include: ATMs nationwide, personal checking, loans and a Visa/ MasterCard at a low APR. For more information call 1-800-347-CCCU.

MUSEUM DISCOUNT

Members can receive discounts for *The Creation Museum* admission purchased on-line. *The Creation Museum* (located in Petersburg, KY) presents a unique and unparalleled experience, a walk through time portraying significant, life-altering events of the past, illuminating the effects of biblical history on our present and future world.

CEAI APP

The app links Christian educators to a plethora of resources.

There are many other benefits and discounts in the marketplace from membership with *CEAI*. However, the greatest benefit is that together we as Christian educators, support staff, parents and friends of education are afforded an opportunity to reach beyond our local areas of influence. As a member of *CEAI*, you are provided the opportunity to network with other believers to impact the very fabric of education in this nation. Together we can help spread the Biblical worldview in action, speech and the written word to impact the lives of the youth we serve.

Core Values

Love
Biblical
Knowledge
Respect
Integrity
Prayer
Patience
Self-control
Worship

Truth
Unity
Forgiveness
Faith
Servanthood
Joy
Professional
Excellence

Statement of Faith

We believe in:

- One God eternally existent in the Father, Son and Holy Spirit.
- The Bible as the inspired Word of God.
- Christ, the Son of God, His virgin birth, His miracles, His vicarious atoning death for our sins, His bodily resurrection and His return.
- The need and reality of spiritual conversion by the Holy Spirit through the death and resurrection of Jesus Christ.
- The ministry of the Holy Spirit Who enables us to live a godly life.

Our Cause

WE R 4 U!

We will invest in Christian educators, members & friends, to find out their call or dream, & encourage, equip, and empower them to walk it out.

Contact:

Membership Service Center
P.O. Box 45610
Westlake, Ohio 44145-1023

Office: 440-250-9566 Email: info@ceai.org
Toll Free: 888-798-1124 Website: ceai.org
Fax: 440-250-9584

Become a Ministry CEAI Partner!

The United States currently has a population of over 313 million people; *CEAI* is looking to partner with a very small percentage of those individuals – 7,000. *Ministry Partners* share their vision that our public schools are in need of transformation and that transformation needs to bubble up locally through educators and friends of education like you.

Ministry Partners commit to support *Christian Educators Association International's* efforts to <u>*transform our schools through God's Love and Truth*</u> financially and in prayer.

CEAI partners will support efforts targeted above and beyond the daily support of our members which is supported by membership fees:

- Enhancing media presence casting the *CEAI* Vision.
- Tackling issues in the courts to assure the religious freedoms of educators, parents, and students.
- Publishing and distributing materials to encourage and equip those outside our membership ranks to openly live out their faith within the schooling culture.
- Conducting workshops and seminars across the country supporting *CEAI's* Mission *To encourage, equip, and empower educators according to Biblical Principles.*

Ministry Partners will be asked …

- To keep the above efforts in prayer and share with those in their sphere of influence about the many issues impacting public education today.
- To make a monthly tax deductable donation of at least $25 to the Ministry of *CEAI.*

CEAI will provide partners with…

- Insider communication about what is happening across the country and locally within the schooling culture and what they are doing about it.
- Access to many of the resources accessible to members (newsletters, magazines, devotionals, and more).

Appendix

To become a CEAI Member and/or a Ministry Partner:

call Toll Free: 888-798-1124
or go to their website: **ceai.org**.

For more information contact:

Finn Laursen
C/O Advantage Books
P.O. Box 160847
Altamonte Springs, FL 32716

info@ advbooks.com

To purchase additional copies of this book or other books
published by Advantage Books call our order number at:

407-788-3110 (Book Orders Only)

or visit our bookstore website at:
www.advbookstore.com

Longwood, Florida, USA
"we bring dreams to life"™
www.advbookstore.com

CPSIA information can be obtained
at www.ICGtesting.com
Printed in the USA
FFOW05n1600131015